KNOCK
...AND STILL THEY COME

Colm Kilcoyne

Knock

...and still they come

the columba press

First published in 2012 by
the columba press
55A Spruce Avenue, Stillorgan Industrial Park,
Blackrock, Co Dublin

Cover by Bill Bolger
Origination by The Columba Press
Printed by MPG Books Ltd, Cornwall

ISBN 978 1 85607 773 6

Contents

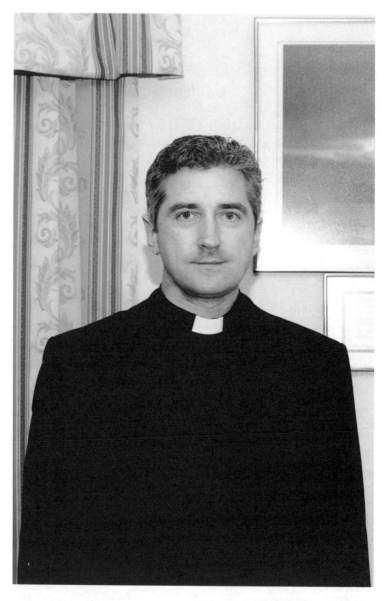

Father Richard Gibbons, Parish Priest, Knock Shrine 2012

FOREWORD

Fr Richard Gibbons, Parish Priest, Knock Shrine

As the new Parish Priest of Knock I am happy to contribute this short piece to Colm Kilcoynes' book on Knock while at the same time acknowledging the sad and sudden death of our former PP, Monsignor Joe Quinn, may he rest in peace.

I was born and raised in Louisburgh, Co Mayo. I attended both primary and secondary school there and then went on to study in UCG (NUIG) where I obtained a degree in Economics and Politics as well as a degree in Law, my intention was to become a solicitor. However, the hand of the Lord being somewhere in the mix, I decided to study for the priesthood and in 1994 was sent to the Irish College in Rome. I was ordained a priest in Louisburgh in 1999 and returned to Rome to finish my post grad studies in 2000. On returning to Ireland, I was appointed curate in Headford, Co Galway as well as chaplain to the Presentation secondary school. While in Headford I completed the H.Dip in Education, qualifying as a secondary school teacher. In 2003 I was appointed curate in Knock and just last week (2nd February 2012) was appointed Parish Priest of Knock and Rector of the National Shrine following the death of Msgr Joe Quinn.

It has been a privilege and honour for me to work in Knock, seeing the various aspects of Christian life played out in a pilgrim context. The searching, the prayers, the tears, the longing for God as well as the fun, joy and thanksgiving on the part of a pilgrim brings home to me the special place that Knock is. The work of the shrine staff as well as the stewards and hand maids makes Knock a welcoming place in the life of a pilgrim. At this stage of my new role in Knock, I will have to take time to explore the current needs of the pilgrim and develop a plan for the future based upon the wonderful foundations of my predecessors – no easy task given the history! However, trusting in the help of Our Lady of Knock, shrine, parish and pilgrim can do no other than forge ahead in faith.

Father Colm Kilcoyne, Editor and Author

INTRODUCTION

In at the deep end

What we see now is like a dim image in a mirror;
then we shall see face to face.
What I know now is only partial;
then it will be complete –
as complete as God's knowledge of me.
1 Cor 13:11

I grew up in a home where there was some but not a lot of devotion to Mary. Other families around us had more, others less. Unusually, it was my father who was more public about his devotion. I cycled with him the forty kilometres from Castlebar to Knock once a year. My mother may have gone more times than I remember but I do know for definite that she was there day the pope came to Knock in 1979.

Her favourite was Blessed Martin de Porres. She knew he was from Peru, that his father was a Spanish noble man, his mother a black woman, that Martin had the looks of his mother. Every so often she'd say he'd have been a saint long since if he was white. He was made a saint eventually in 1962. Nearly 400 years after he was born. A delay that only fuelled her theory.

Oliver Plunkett was my father's man. Him and St Joseph. Oliver Plunkett because of his martyrdom at Tyburn in London. The Brits again. St Joseph because he was a quiet man and a good provider. Not unlike my father himself. In our house, as you can see, saints were honoured for reasons other than their sanctity. This meant Our Lady struggled for attention.

An odd time we'd have the rosary – usually because my father would have been to the mission, the priest would have talked about the family rosary and how every home should have it. So, we'd have the rosary for the few nights but somehow it always seemed to fade away after that.

In 1985, when I was 51 years old I was appointed curate in

Knock. Some would see a quirky providence at work in the appointment. I didn't. But there I was. A fish out of water.

I had come to Knock nervous of devotion to Mary. Hadn't we Jesus and his gospels? What devotions could be better than the parables? Doesn't every parent get the point of The Prodigal Son? Everyone with a heart understand The Good Samaritan?

At the Last Supper didn't the washing of the feet teach us all we needed to know about care for each other? Wasn't it enough that Jesus left us the Eucharist to nourish our journey as Christians? Why dilute the centrality of Jesus?

That was the baggage I brought to Knock.

This chapter maps a path from our kitchen to where I am now in Marian devotion. How listening to Knock pilgrims gave me some understanding of the part played by Mary in the story of Jesus and as a result her place in our story as Christians. All the while remembering and respecting people like my parents who walk a different path.

I arrived at a time when Msgr James Horan was in his element. Flat out developing the physical structure of Knock. He built the Basilica (1976) to shelter up to 10,000 pilgrims. When people criticised its plainness he'd tell them it was meant to be a large umbrella, nothing more, nothing less and umbrellas are designed not for looks but to stop people getting wet. So there.

It wasn't just bricks and mortar. Just when garden centres and pretty lawns were getting popular Msgr Horan landscaped the hundred acre shrine site. Today the beauty and colour of the grounds are a significant part of the serenity of the Knock experience.

The airport was a twinkle in his eye long before he cajoled, badgered, schemed and eventually wore down officialdom into backing his dream. The airport, built on 'the foggy , boggy hill' opened in May 1986.

Two months after its opening Msgr Horan went as a pilgrim to Lourdes from Knock Airport. He died there suddenly on 1 August 1986. His was the first coffin to come into the new Knock airport. His airport.

He was a one-off. A driven, talented man with a vision for the west. Problems only fuelled his energy. Or so I thought. When he died I got to meet a close relation of his. I mentioned the intense dedication to his projects and his indifference to opposition. This relation looked at me and said perhaps there was something I should know.

Msgr Horan did worry. He worried a lot. Many a time when this relation visited him in the evenings he had serious doubts about his projects. Frightened at the thought of failure.

This was the Msgr James Horan who did a famous RTÉ interview with Jim Fahy standing on the foundations of the airport. At his flamboyant best: the trademark Russian hat, arms stretched wide, the big laugh and confident predictions about the airport.

To think that on the evenings of days like that Msgr Horan may have shed anxious tears.

One of the regrets of my time in Knock is that I hadn't seen this side of Msgr Horan. He was so busy. So out there. So full of ideas and building projects. His public style told me Msgr Horan didn't do doubt. Not only that but he wouldn't have much time for doubt in others. I was wrong.

So, I used to go out on the grounds, sit on a seat and wait until a pilgrim sat beside me. Life had taught me that when the clerical wing of the church is hard going there is great wisdom and still greater kindness in most lay people. They are less absolute, more at ease with mess. More tuned to their own confusion and more inclined to respect it in others.

I'd sit there. A pilgrim would come up and ask if they could join me. Of course.

They had time to talk. Where they were from. Who was at home. What brought them to Knock. What the day had been like. Lives were opened up and talked about simply, softly and eloquently.

What had helped? The peace. Being away for the few hours. Meeting people in the same boat as themselves. Each with a story to tell. Sharing worries. Sickness. Trouble at home. Tired of trying to cope. Tired of failing. Yes, the few hours at Knock had been a great help. Meeting others – complete strangers – was good.

I was finding that the telling and the listening were a huge part of the gift that Knock has to offer pilgrims. Not just them but myself as well.

That was then. Now in this book, seventeen years after leaving Knock, I am revisiting it. I dip a little into the Knock that was back then but mainly I try to let today's Knock talk. I hope I do justice to it because Knock now has the potential to nourish not just pilgrims but the Irish church. A church that is changing before our eyes.

There are people who want their church to be relevant to themselves and their children but somehow life as they experience it and church as they find it just don't match up. They are hanging in but are frustrated, annoyed and critical.

This wing of the church, I feel, is growing by the day. These are not people who want to pull the house down. They just want to be in a church that's awake, that cares and that puts a bit of energy and creativity into how to live the gospel. A church that trusts its message and trusts people. When they leave they won't create a fuss. At that stage they are past bothering.

This is relevant to Knock. It has the potential to be a place where the needs of the human spirit are met by a church that's aware of its treasures and knows how to share them. You will read in some chapters of this book that Knock is already moving into areas of spirituality that are new to Knock but as old as Christianity. This is a sign of hope not just for Knock but for our parishes and the whole Irish church.

I thank all who were so helpful with ideas and interviews. Thanks to Mr Pat Lavelle, Knock Shrine Manager, and his staff for organising some of the practicalities in putting this book together. Mention must also be made of the many staff who work on the grounds and behind the scenes to create the atmosphere that makes the Knock Shrine so pleasant to visit. My gratitude to The Columba Press for asking me to do this. Whatever benefits the book may be to others, it has helped me face and make peace with some memories. Which is what Knock at its best, does best.

Candlelight Procession at Knock Shrine

The Parish Church at Knock Shrine

CHAPTER ONE

An Interview with
The Late Msgr Joe Quinn PP Knock
and Rector of Knock Shrine

Msgr Joe Quinn was among the first I talked to about this book. Partly out of courtesy but mostly because I knew of his love for Knock Shrine and everything about it.

So many tributes have been paid to him since his sudden death in November 2011. All richly deserved. My memory is of a priest who never wanted to be other than a priest. It showed in his enthusiasm for church things. It blossomed in his time in Knock.

Not long before he died he gave me this interview for this book. All that was likeable about Msgr Joe Quinn comes through in his words.

My sister still has a picture of our Lady that hung in our house when we were young. If you look closely you will see that the bottom of the frame is very slightly scorched. That's because our mother used to light a candle before the picture if there ever was anything she wanted Our Lady's help for. When you are young and see things like that you are going to grow up with a familiarity with Mary. To this day I have a statue of Our Lady in my house and I don't mind admitting that I talk to Mary in passing as I would to my own mother and ask for any help I need.

We had the Rosary at night in our home. We went to Sunday evening devotions in Castlebar. At one stage they were doing up Our Lady's side chapel in the church. My grandmother had a huge interest in what was happening. Every week out of her pension she paid towards the renovation. There was something there that said to me that Mary was family.

I got ordained just when Vatican II seemed to be saying that some of the traditional devotions to Mary were outdated. Old fashioned. So there was a pretty clean sweep out of statues and devotions from our churches. With time the pendulum has swung back and we are seeing more balance.

My interest in Knock was always there but a project of Msgr Horan brought me into practical contact with the workings of Knock shrine. While he was working on building the Basilica he had plans to have a novena as soon as it was finished. But he had no structure, no set novena prayers for the nine days. I had done a liturgy course at Carlow so I was roped in to help with the literature and the shape of the novena. The novena ran from 14 to 22 August. From the vigil of the Feast of the Assumption to the day after the date of the apparition. Today the novena attracts around 100,000 pilgrims.

In September 2002 I was appointed parish priest of Knock. It was life-changing to put it mildly. I knew the history of the apparition and never had any doubt about its veracity. I knew about the pilgrimages because I had been on many. But being here day after day and meeting pilgrims I found out a few things. Especially why most pilgrims come to Knock.

Time after time I heard 'peace.' 'I get peace here.' So many living the opposite of peace. Turmoil in the house, turmoil in their hearts. But step onto the grounds, they said, and you sense you are among people who are going through what you are.

They say Irish people have a natural sense of pilgrimage. We had sacred places before Christianity came. They were incorpor - ated into Christianity. There's a big sense of touch in Celtic spirit - uality. You can see that in a stream of pilgrims touching the stone from the original apparition gable wall.

Are there miracles at Knock? We apply the same strict rules

that all shrines do. There may or may not be miracles as we understand them but to receive the grace to cope with whatever is bothering the pilgrim is its own miracle.

We do the liturgy well. On solemn occasions Mass in the Basilica is an experience that invites the congregation into a sense of the mystery and the transcendent. There are moments when you feel the thousands of pilgrims melting into an awareness that they are there with the same mission. All walking the same journey. All being absorbed into the potential for healing that is every Mass.

I would argue that Knock will be pivotal in the renewal of the Irish church. That is a big claim but I stand over it. Whatever shape or form that renewal takes it will be based on two pillars of spirituality.

One pillar of renewal will have to be a return to the sacramental life of the church. That means Mass, the sacrament of reconciliation, the sacrament of the sick. As supplements to these sacraments we will need to recover respect for devotions like the rosary, the Stations of the Cross, prayer guidance, counselling. The other pillar of church renewal that Knock can promote is the study and praying of the scriptures. We are trying to respond to those two challenges.

1. *As regards the sacraments:*
• The sacrament of the Eucharist is both central to the apparition and is the highlight of the pilgrimage day.
• Over 5000 pilgrims a week receive the sacrament of Recon - ciliation at Knock.
• When you come to Knock the visit opens you to reflect on your life. That may lead you to the sacrament of Reconciliation. Or it may bring on feelings that there are issues, not material for the sacrament, that you would like to face now. That is where our trained counsellors provide a wonderful service. You will find this facility near the Chapel of Reconciliation. You can make an appointment but if you find yourself on the grounds and feel you would like to meet a counsellor you can just drop in. No appointment. You just drop in.
• I believe the counselling facility is an essential part of the healing of the spirit that a place like Knock should specialise in.

• The sick have always have a special place at Knock. So many pilgrims are broken, reaching out to God for healing. The sacrament of the Anointing of the Sick is understood nowadays not just as the sacrament of the dying but of sickness in all its shapes and forms. It is a sacrament of healing. This quality of Knock is summed up in the opening prayer to Our Lady of Knock: 'Our Lady of Knock Queen of Peace. You gave hope to your people in a time of distress.' That is still true.

2. As regards scripture
Knock is also about understanding and praying the scriptures. The apparition shows St John with a copy of the scriptures in his hand. He is teaching from it. To be true to that element of the apparition we must take scripture seriously at Knock.
• We hear a lot about our weak Catholic understanding of the bible. Well, here at Knock the shrine bookshop has a busy scripture unit. A sign that pilgrims understand the importance of knowing more about scripture. Not just having knowledge of scripture but using it as a source of prayer and day to day Christening living. 'Faith seeking understanding.'
• The guided prayer ministry at the shrine has 16,000 participants a year. This ministry includes training in praying the scripture as well as spiritual direction. Providing this facility is based on the conviction that scripture is the second of two indispensable strands of renewal along with the other pillar – the sacraments, especially Mass.

The future
• The Basilica opened in 1976. It has given sturdy service. The time may be now to refurbish the interior.
• They talk about the lost generation, 20-40 year olds – young people who somehow missed out on seeing the importance of faith and practising that faith. The popularity of the Youth Ministry at Knock and the decent percentage of young people at special events at Knock give great hope. We run youth retreats and will continue to give attention to this important group.

CHAPTER TWO

The story of the Apparition

Taken from the Official Knock Shrine literature

The 15 Official Witnesses
1. Dominick Byrne (senior), Drum, Knock, aged thirty-six years
2. Dominick Byrne (junior), Drum, Knock, aged twenty years approximately
3. Margaret Byrne, Drum, Knock, aged twenty-one years
4. Mary Byrne, Drum, Knock, aged twenty-nine years approximately
5. Mrs Margaret Byrne (widow), Drum, Knock, aged sixty-eight years
6. Patrick Byrne, Carrowmore, Knock, aged sixteen years
7. Judith Campbell, Carrowmore, Knock, aged twenty-two years
8. John Curry, Lecarrow, Knock, aged five years
9. John Durkan, casual labourer, aged twenty-four years approximately
10. Mrs Hugh Flatley, Cloonlee, Knock, aged forty-four years
11. Patrick Hill, Claremorris, aged eleven years
12. Mary McLoughlin, Archdeacon Cavanagh's housekeeper, Knock, aged forty-five years
13. Catherine Murray, Lisaniskea, Bekan, aged eight years
14. Bridget Trench, Carrowmore, Knock, aged seventy-four years approximately
15. Patrick Walsh, Ballindorris, Knock, aged sixty-five years approximately

FIRST COMMISSION OF ENQUIRY, 1879

Mary Byrne's Testimony
Archbishop John Mc Hale of Tuam set up a Commission of Enquiry in 1879. All fifteen of the witnesses were examined. The

commission reported to the archbishop that the testimony of all, taken as a whole, was 'trustworthy and satisfactory'.

Mary Byrne's testimony gives a flavour of the detail the witnesses gave to the commission:

I live in the village of Knock, to the east side of the chapel. Mary McLoughlin came on the evening of 21 August to my house at about half past seven o'clock. She remained some little time.

I came back with her as she was returning homewards. It was either eight o'clock or a quarter to eight at the time. It was still bright. I had not heard from Miss McLoughlin about the vision which she had seen just before that.

The first I learned of it was on coming at the time just named from my mother's house in company with Miss Mary McLoughlin, and at the distance of three hundred yards or so from the church. I beheld, all at once, standing out from the gable, and rather to the west of it, three figures which, on more attentive inspection, appeared to be that of the Blessed Virgin, St Joseph and St John. That of the Blessed Virgin was life-size, the others apparently either not so big or not so high as her figure.

They stood a little distance out from the gable wall and, as well as I could judge, a foot and a half or two feet from the ground.

The Virgin stood erect, with eyes raised to heaven, her hands elevated to the shoulders or a little higher, the palms inclined slightly towards the shoulders or bosom. She wore a large cloak of a white colour, hanging in full folds and some-what loosely around her shoulders, and fastened to the neck. She wore a crown on the head, rather a large crown, and it appeared to me somewhat yellower than the dress or robes worn by Our Blessed Lady.

In the figure of St Joseph the head was slightly bent, and inclined towards the Blessed Virgin, as if paying her respect. It represented the saint as somewhat aged, with grey whiskers and greyish hair.

The third figure appeared to be that of St John the Evangelist. I do not know, only I thought so, except the fact that at one time I saw a statue at the chapel of Lecanvey, near

Westport, Co Mayo, very much resembling the figure which stood now before me in group with St Joseph and Our Blessed Lady, which I beheld on this occasion.

He held the Book of Gospels, or the Mass Book, open in his left hand, while he stood slightly turned on the left side towards the altar that was over a little from him. I must remark that the statue which I had formerly seen at Lecanvey chapel had no mitre on its head, while the figure which now beheld had one, not a high mitre, but a short set kind of one. The statue at Lecanvey had a book in his left hand, and the fingers of the right hand raised. The figure before me on this present occasion of which I am speaking had a book in the left hand, as I stated, and the index finger and the middle finger of the right hand raised, as if he were speaking, and impressing some point forcibly on an audience. It was this coincidence of figure and pose that made me surmise, for it is only an opinion, that the third figure was that of St John, the beloved disciple of Our Lord, but I am not in any way sure what saint or character the figure represented. I said, as I now expressed, that it was St John the Evangelist, and then all the others present said what I stated.

The altar was under the window, which is in the gable and a little to the west near the centre, or a little beyond it. Towards this altar St John, as I shall call the figure, was looking, while he stood at the gospel side of the said altar, which his right arm inclined at an angle outwardly, towards the Blessed Virgin. The altar appeared to be like the altars in use in the Catholic Church, large and full-sized. It had no linens, no candles, nor any special ornamentations; it was only a plain altar.

Above the altar and resting on it was a lamb and around it I saw golden stars, or small brilliant lights, glittering like jets or glass balls, reflecting the light of some luminous body.

I remained from a quarter past eight to half past nine o'clock. At the time it was raining.

SECOND COMMISSION OF ENQUIRY 1936

Mary Byrne's Testimony

By now there were just three of the witnesses alive. John Curry who had gone to America. His testimony was taken there. Patrick Byrne and Mary Byrne still lived in Ireland. Mary was eighty-six at the time of the second Commission of Enquiry. She was interviewed by the commissioners in her bedroom, as she was too ill to leave. She gave her final testimony on oath and concluded with the words:

> I am clear about everything I have said and I make this statement knowing I am going before my God.

Mary died six weeks later.

The commission spent three years completing its work. The verdict: 'The evidence of the witnesses was upright and trustworthy.'

CHAPTER THREE

Popular Devotions and Knock
Fr Colm Kilcoyne

All the places in our lives are sacred.
Just that some have steeples.
Robert Benson

What do we mean by Popular Devotions?
God is the great mystery. If knowing him were easy, religion
would be easy. Which means we should be humble about our
capacity to know God or fully express him in this or that set of
words or ritual. So much of the infinite is beyond our finite abil-
ity. We will always fall short.

Take the Eucharist. Central to our faith is the presence of
Christ in the Word spoken, the bread broken. I find it easy to believe that, to totally accept its truth and relevance to my life. But
I would be very worried if I ever reached the point were I
thought I was clever and articulate enough to assemble wads of
words to explain the Eucharist. At that stage I'd have reduced
mystery to grammar. A kind of blasphemy.

Which brings us to popular devotions. Their strength and at-
traction for so many is they recognise there are truths beyond
the reach of words. So mostly they bypass words. The Knock apparition itself. Look at holy wells, holy mountains, holy water.
All of them involve actions and you know what they say about
actions speaking louder than words.

Take the Knock apparition. No words were spoken. But like
children growing in the faith, Knock started with devotions.
People just came and said whatever prayers they wanted in
whatever order they wished. There was no set routine. It was
your typical people-driven devotion. A popular devotion.

Devotions tune us to mystery. The problem is that one person's devotion becomes another's superstition, which is why the
church has always been nervous that popular devotions might
contaminate official liturgies and doctrines. Of course it makes
sense to keep an eye on popular piety. But it makes bigger sense

to recognise that God doesn't speak only through defined doctrine and church officials. Jesus used all kinds of props to tell his
story. Fifty-seven parables. All about familiar things and situations. He also used some unlikely people to work through. Still
does.

They are called popular devotions or popular pieties because
they are of and from the people. For whatever reason people in
some part of the world adopt a particular devotion. It takes root.
The official church may or may not give the devotion its blessing. That doesn't seem to matter. The devotion persists despite
official coolness. Indeed sometimes you suspect it thrives pre-
cisely because of official coolness.

What I am talking about are apparitions, Divine Mercy, the
Child of Prague, St Anthony, the Blue Rosary, Stations of the
Cross, blessings, statues, novenas, relics, medals, holy water,
holy wells, holy candles, holy saints , holy mountains, May processions. And many, many more. All are of the people.

We can take or leave devotions. We are not necessarily better
or worse Catholics because of our attitude to them. We can ignore them as many do. Or we can make them an important part
of our spirituality. Again, as many do.

The most unlikely people share devotions. Take Tom Crean
and Pope John Paul II. Tom Crean was a Kerryman who was an
Antarctic explorer. There's a great one man show/play that tells
his story. He travelled with other heroes like Shackleton and
Scott. Both record in their diaries that Tom Crean always wore
the Brown Scapular around his neck. Popular piety saw the
scapular as a protection against danger As it happened Tom
Crean survived where many died. His death came many years
later, back in the serenity of Kerry where he ran a pub called The
South Pole Inn.

When Pope John Paul II was shot and operated on in 1981 he told
doctors not to remove the Brown Scapular he was wearing. He had been
wearing the scapular since his First Communion in Poland and wore
one until he died in 2005. That was twenty four years after the shooting.

Two men from opposite ends of Europe and from different
Catholic traditions at one in their intuition that there is more to
faith than we can express in doctrines or liturgies. That there is a
space for popular devotions.

Because devotions are ranked lower than our core beliefs doesn't mean they are unimportant. Far from it. The best of the devotions prepare us for those deeper truths.

Take the Sacred Heart picture that hung in every Catholic kitchen. The one with the eyes that followed you. You could be a know all and say this was down to the trick of a clever artist. We knew that, thanks very much, but we also knew, in some incoherent way, that it was about a bigger truth.

As we grew up we heard more about that bigger truth. The gospel of Matthew: Are not two sparrows sold for a penny yet not one sparrow falls to the ground without your heavenly Father knowing it? Jesus reassuring us that the God of the universe is also the God of small things. We are in the eye of a caring God. Then it clicks. So that is what the roving eye of the Sacred Heart picture was trying to teach us.

Here we have a devotion, a piece of popular piety doing what popular piety does well. It starts as a holy picture on a kitchen wall. Baby food preparing us for some later understanding of the presence of God in all his creation.

Childhood memories of these devotions and images are powerful. Their touch, smell and sensual nature respect a child's way of learning. They are important elements in the menu of folk religion. They ready the spirit for the official church menu of sacraments and the core doctrines of our faith.

The Knock apparition: A devotion leading us to the core of our faith.

As time went by the Knock apparition was studied more carefully. Take St John holding a book of scripture. This at a time (the 1880s) when the bible was divisive in the west. Memories of Bible Schools and soup kitchens were still fresh. Edward Nangle, the founder of the Achill Mission, only died four years after the apparition. This piece of recent history made some Catholics see the bible as a Protestant thing. Its absence from Catholic homes was taken as a sign by Nangle that those Catholics badly needed saving. The bible was, to put it mildly, divisive in Tuam diocese. Knock is part of that diocese.

And yet here is the Knock apparition happening right smack in the middle of that bible controversy. St John looking us in the eye and teaching from the open book of scripture. More or less telling us to grow up, stop being prisoners of foolish disputes and recognise scripture for what it is. Not a book for churches to squabble over but the Word of God and an essential source of spirituality for all Christians.

I find that probably the most impressive part of the apparition scene. It was a command to embrace the bible. Something many Catholics had come to see as a weapon to make them change their religion. The apparition was asking people to look deeper into their tradition and recover the reverence for scripture that showed in their Celtic prayers and manuscripts.

It is for each of us to answer how loyal we have been to that particular part of the apparition. How much attention we pay to the Liturgy of the Word at Mass. How influential are the words and actions of Jesus in my words and actions?

It is at this point that devotion bows to solid doctrine. We may pray all we wish at the apparition gable but we aren't ready to leave until we do so with some determination to live in our daily lives the values in that book St John is holding.

People of faith come to Knock. A million and a half of them. They come in all shapes and sizes, all levels of faith, all with their own history, all with different relationship with church and God. All with a life after they go home from Knock. They belong to homes and parishes .

A day in Knock is not a day in a bubble. It is a day of nourishment for life back home. Knock's challenge is to give the pilgrim the spiritual experiences that will help him or her in their personal and family lives. It will have done a good job if the pilgrim goes home energised enough to be active in the renewal of our tired church. Active also in community projects that might do for today what the Knock prayer says the apparition did for life back then: 'gave hope to people in their time of distress'.

CHAPTER FOUR

Irish Marian Devotion
Fr Colm Kilcoyne

I have the good mother of God for a sister
Donncha Mór, 13th century

At the time of the apparition in 1879 the prayers of the people – whether in Irish or English – still had a distinctive intimate language when addressing Mary. This means we are looking at a generation influenced by the special Celtic understanding of who Mary was.

In those prayers Mary is seen as a mother close to her children in their needs. Those needs were basic. Sick stock, sick children, poor crops, poverty . You could look at those prayers and wonder why they aren't about more spiritual things. That's to forget that when you are desperate there is a thin enough line between the secular and the sacred. Indeed when you think of it Christianity itself fudges that line with the incarnation, the Word made flesh in Christ.

Down the centuries the official church had developed a male edge. Its rules and regulations were the products of the male mind. A forest of scaffolding surrounding, protecting, isolating and fencing off the Jesus of the gospels.

This left Irish Catholics with a wall of doctrine between themselves and the Jesus of the gospels. What that wall couldn't do was isolate the people from Mary . Popular piety – especially the prayers of those pieties – pictured Mary as a mother, softer than the Son the church had projected. She was as accessible as your rosary beads. The mother that suffered. The mother who stood by her son. A Mary we could relate to.

In an Ireland of landlords, bailiffs, evictions and poverty, people had learned to survive by knowing those who were kind and understood sickness, hunger and misery. Those with no power or influence must work through those who have. Mary was such a person.

Jesus was seen as the child of Mary's womb. In the prayers he was always *Mac Mhuire*, Mary's son. Known through his

mother the way we'd know a neighbour's child. This style re-
spected the importance of the mother as well as the son in the
story of our redemption.

Some have described the place of Mary in popular Irish
Catholic spirituality as a member of the extended family. A pilgrim
from the Knock area told me that her mother had such familiarity
with Mary that she walked and talked with her as if she was her
sister and mother. Donncha Mór said the same thing as far back
as the 13th century: 'I have the good mother of God for a sister.'
Mary as family.

That, I believe, is why so many pilgrims have a connection
with Mary. Their understanding of suffering is mutual. She suffered. They suffer. She and they are family, with all the casual
intimacy, the absence of deference, the shared history that family
members have.

In Irish Catholic spirituality the way of achieving union with
God through Christ was seen as easier when done with and
through Mary. There was a belief that through Mary we would
receive the mercy of God rather than his anger. She would put
in a good word for us at the right time and in the right place.
And if that sounds too corny think of the wedding feast of Cana.

Hospitality had been a pre-Christian Celtic virtue. Irish Christian
spirituality gave it the same importance. It identified generosity of spirit
as the engine of hospitality. Mary's visitation of her cousin Elizabeth and
her rescue of the wedding couple at Cana were models of the warm
heartedness and generous spirit that should mark all Christians.

Suffering for its own sake was not part of Celtic Christian
spirituality. Suffering would yield meaning only if we could see
it as some sort of sharing in the passion of Christ. And what
made that idea tolerable for the rest of us was knowing that this
is also how Mary saw suffering.

We walk together with the Virgin Mary and the other holy
people who accompanied her only Son on the hill of Calvary.
Diarmuid Ó Laoghaire offers a poem that makes Mary central to
the passion. It is called *Caoineadh na dTrí Mhuire (The Lament of
the three Marys)*. Jesus is in the depths of his passion. The poem
has Mary say to Jesus: 'My child, your burden is great. Let your
Mother share part of it.' Mary at the heart of the redemptive act
and not just a sympathetic mother standing by.

Importantly, this also means that you and I are committed by baptism to carry our share – like Mary – not just of the historic passion of Christ but the passion as experienced today by people demeaned by poverty, oppression or prejudice. What nowadays we'd call social justice. Back then it meant *muintearas* – community, neighbourliness, hospitality, responsibility for each other and for nature. The examples held up to imitate in all these areas of life were Jesus and Mary.

All of which means, I suggest, that Marian devotions for our people were meaningless unless they had an influence on how we behaved with each other. The test was not our prayers but our actions. That is still the test.

You know as well as I do that there are all kinds of names for people who are full of piety but difficult to be around. A true story. A woman who was fierce holy, prayed and complained in equal measures all day every day. She got bad and this time the end really was close. She was still complaining. But she also found the strength to tell them she believed her agony was nearly over and soon she would be going home to spend eternity with her beloved God. To which someone around the bed whispered: 'Poor God.'

I tell this not at the expense of well-meaning people but because many of us are tempted to separate our prayers from the realities of our lives.

A way of correcting that is to remember a moment in Mary's life. She is in prayer when the annunciation occurs. She immediately applies the news to the reality of her life. 'How can this happen since I am a virgin?' And then she realises her own good news should impel her to be with her cousin Elizabeth.

Mary's prayer life has sensitised her to see its implications for her own life and the needs of the people in her life. There is a sense in which prayer starts when it ends.

By now many of us may have lost any connection with the lovely ease and intimacy of the older Irish Catholic Marian prayers. But the basic question about prayer is still the same: If prayer isn't about being life-changing what is it about?

Fr John J. Ó Ríordáin's book *Irish Catholic Spirituality* (Columba Press) and Fr Frank Fahy's booklet *The Rosary Way* (privately published) are excellent sources on Irish Marian spirituality. I am indebted to both.

Tom Neary, Chief Steward at Knock Shrine

CHAPTER FIVE

Tom Neary: Chief Steward at Knock

Some argue places like Knock make too much of Mary.
Look at the Apparition Chapel. The altar highlighting the
Eucharist is more central than she is.
Mass is the centre and high point of the Knock devotions.

Knock Shrine Society of Handmaids and Stewards, founded in 1935, is
a voluntary body and its members are committed to serving the church
at Knock. They come from all over Ireland, from all walks of life and
from all age groups. Those who are 18 years of age and not more than
55 can apply to become registered members. Those under 18 years of
age can join the Youth Section.

The stewards help to keep order at the shrine during large pilgrim-
ages, on Saturdays and Sundays and for special events. They form and
lead the processions, participate in the liturgical ceremonies, act as
Ministers of the Eucharist and assist the sick, elderly and those with
special needs.

I was born two miles from Knock. The older people around
me knew the story in great detail. The very old people knew the
visionaries in person and some were relations. They'd quote the
witnesses saying 'We saw what we saw and we told exactly
what we saw as it was.'

One of my own relations, John Coyne, a young man, went to
the village to collect letters the day of the apparition. He rode a
horse. He passed by the church and saw the apparition. He
came home, said nothing because he didn't know what it was.
The next day it was all over the place and then he talked. He
wasn't recognised as an official witness when the commission
took place because he had emigrated to the US at that stage.

When I was young in the 1940s there was a great religious
atmosphere. Holy pictures. The May altar. Mass was very important . We had the rosary and did the stations. I often saw pilgrims doing their pilgrimage on their knees. Connemara people

wore shawls. Knock would be packed with bikes, carts, buses, side cars and traps. CIE buses would be parked a few miles along the road.

14 August was a huge day. It was the eve of the Feast of the Assumption. Pilgrims walked all evening and all night by our house. I can member the noise, the sound of boots and sticks on the road. Some walked from as far away as Roscommon.

I went to college but there was still the pull of Knock. There was no youth culture at the time. Young and old mixed in. No sense that when you reached the teenage years you should break away from the way you were reared.

We still practised what we now call a simple faith. It might be simple but it was profound. A sense of the presence of God. A sense that there was right and there was wrong and the job of a Christian was to live right.

To do that we prayed and then did our best to live it out in our day-to-day daily lives. Crowds in Knock would stand in the rain and mud. There was no tar under foot. I remember that vividly. It was moving for a young person to see what older people put up with because of their faith.

In time I became a steward at Knock and then chief steward. It has been a great experience. I met people that impressed me. Big names like Pope John Paul II, Fr Pat Peyton and Mother Teresa. I also met hundreds and hundreds of good people and the more I got to know them the more their goodness rubbed off on me.

Meantime my own family was growing. I have to say that one nice thing in my life is that they too have found inspiration in the shrine and what it stands for. We never had any problem with them growing up about not going to church or living their faith. It is a happy moment for any Catholic parents to find that what he or she sees important in religion is now also important to their family.

And indeed they now have their own families and the interest and commitment to the faith has passed on to them. I give the credit for all that to the unique atmosphere, the example of pilgrims and the challenge to live the gospel you get when you come to Knock.

My favourite place on the shrine grounds is the Apparition Chapel. The heart of Knock is there. What you see in the position and stance of the statues is very very close to the original scene. You see the essential aspects of Knock. Spend time there and it will remind you of the basics of our faith.

At the centre is the Eucharist scene. You have the altar and the Lamb on it. You have Mary inviting all to not just look at the altar of the Eucharist but to take part ourselves in the Eucharist. St John has the bible open and is clearly teaching from it. A reminder, maybe that the people back then and ever since should pay more heed to scripture. Quietly overlooking the whole scene is St Joseph.

Millions have come here with faith problems, health problems, relationship problems. And many to give thanks. When visitors have something special about them something of their presence lingers when they are gone. That is certainly true when you sit or kneel in the Apparition Chapel. You feel something of the original apparition but also of the millions who have prayed their hearts out here.

People who come have faith of some kind. It may be strong. It may be weak. But it is there. In general you can presume they believe in God to some degree and are church members – again to some degree. When they gather they create a definite atmosphere. People feel free to connect with the spiritual because that is what people do here.

So if I pray at Knock I will be at home here. The place invites it. Other pilgrims by praying invite it. An awful lot come with petitions. Some mundane, some serious, all the things we talk about with someone we trust

I know some say this is religion at a very basic level. Not very sophisticated. I know it doesn't necessarily make the person making the petitions more spiritual or easier to live. But pilgrims see Knock as a place where they can bring that worry to somebody who can help. It is pretty straightforward and simple if you wish but it is also very direct and it shows an ease with the spiritual.

There is an old Celtic thing, Mary as mother. The feminine with all the intuitive understanding and sensitivity that the title carries with it. Mary sometimes has the title of queen but I feel Mother gives her an intimacy and immediacy that needs no explaining. You can call it unsophisticated if you wish but you could also say it is a remarkable awareness of the continuity between the material and the spiritual. That the heart has no boundaries. That Jesus through Mary is still concerned with the concerns the gospels tell us he concerned himself with. The people Jesus met in his own day had basic needs too.

Some argue places like Knock make too much of Mary. That it puts her central. My answer is that Knock doesn't make her central. Look at the Apparition Chapel. The altar highlighting the Eucharist is more central than she is. Take the pilgrimage on any given day. Mass is the centre and high point of the Knock devotions. It is where all the elements of the pilgrimage co me together.

Not all pilgrims come to beg favours. Many come to say thanks. In fact it is interesting that many who work here do so because it is their way of saying thanks.

Many foreigners come – Polish, Indians, Moroccan, Nigerian. I notice they have a special reverence about them when they are here. A gentility. A graciousness. More and more there are special days and special rituals for them.

I get asked what kind of Christians does Knock hope to produce. I'd say number one would be help pilgrims realise that their faith and gospel living is number one. To do that we must see the place of prayer but we must also respect nature, care for the sick, use the sacraments. Our dream at Knock is to be a place that reminds pilgrims of what is core in Christian living. Not only that, but provide them with the nourishment that will help them live those basic Christians qualities when they go home.

A final point. Knock at its nicest around 8-9 in the evening. It is quiet and peaceful on the grounds and around the flower-beds. It soothes the spirit. I find it hard to imagine people being attracted to church if you haven't a nice setting. Atmosphere matters. Knock has it.

CHAPTER SIX

The Chapel of Reconciliation
Fr Colm Kilcoyne

Let not your heart be troubled, neither let it be afraid.
(John 14:27)

The Chapel of Reconciliation was built in 1989. A huge addition not just to the physical facilities at Knock but to what you might call the soul of a place of pilgrimage. People come on pilgrimage for many reasons. High on the list, I suspect, are frayed relationships and worries about where the pilgrim stands with God.

The chapel, deliberately called the Chapel of Reconciliation, is meant to give penitents the experience of talking out what they feel needs healing. Of making peace with a sometimes needlessly tortured past.

The sacrament of Reconciliation has taken several forms down the centuries. Many of us were reared in the form where most of the sacrament happened in the confessional box. An exercise in self-accusation followed by absolution.

For several years now there has been an emphasis on the sacrament as a journey home to our truest selves. Where we reflect on our lives in the hours, maybe the days, ahead of the sacrament. We look at our relationship with God, with people, with ourselves (eg how do we use our gifts and time?).

Ideally, at some stage we hit a Prodigal Son moment. Where the desire to be home becomes greater than the reasons for staying as we are. Where we move from what we have to say and how we will say it to wanting to experience what the Prodigal Son must have when he heard his father say: 'This son of mine was dead but now he is alive; he was lost but now he has been found.'

That story is embedded in us ever since we first heard it. It provides the single most powerful motivation for using the sacrament of Reconciliation. Over 5000 pilgrims a week do so during the pilgrimage season.

The first time you go to Knock you may find it hard enough to see the Chapel of Reconciliation although is right there on front of you. That's because part of it is under ground level. The roof connects the eye with the hill behind it and the fourteen Stations of the Cross on that hill.

You leave the shrine on ground level and go into the chapel down a short avenue. It gives you a feeling of having made a decision like the Prodigal Son did. He came to his senses and said: 'I will arise and go to my Father's house' (Lk 15).

The interior is as much an invitation to reconciliation as is humanly possible. The mood is perfect. You come away, up the slope and back into the day-to-day world, having heard the words of absolution: 'May God give you pardon and peace.'

Sometimes we go to the sacrament with a story we really want to sort out. We think we are ready this time. We go in, do our best but when we come out and sit in the seat we feel we've just talked the headlines. Leaving the confessional we were wished 'pardon and peace' but we still aren't at peace.

The first thing to be said is that this is common. Also it almost certainly has been 'a good confession'.

After that I can do no better than turn to the insights of Sr Angela Forde. For a time she was Director of The Counselling Centre at Knock. In summary she says this:

> While many find solace and healing in the sacrament, the confessors at Knock over the years have become increasingly aware that some individual penitents needed more and more expertise than they could provide in the confessional.

> Some of the problems they met were not necessarily of a confessional nature but needed attention if the penitent was to experience God's forgiveness and healing. Since the care of the whole person is at the core of what Knock is about, this led to the provision of the Counselling Service.

> This service means that if they wish those who have received the sacrament and still do not feel at peace with themselves or others can explore the problem in more depth. They can be helped to understand that what is framed as a spiritual problem has a human dimension and that it is only as the human issues are unravelled that we can be truly open to the spiritual.

She gives an example: 'I cannot pray contemplatively any more' has very little to do with prayer but much more with the ungrieved loss of a loved one.
(*The Meaning of Knock*, Columba Press, p 76 - 79)

So what you have at Knock is a variety of ways of 'telling your story'. You can talk it in confession, in the counselling room, to people you meet on the grounds, in a chapel or on the grounds, or mulling over it yourself. These all have the potential to feed into each other and nourish the pilgrim's spirit. Whichever way or combination of ways you chose is part of the process of healing . That is God's gift.

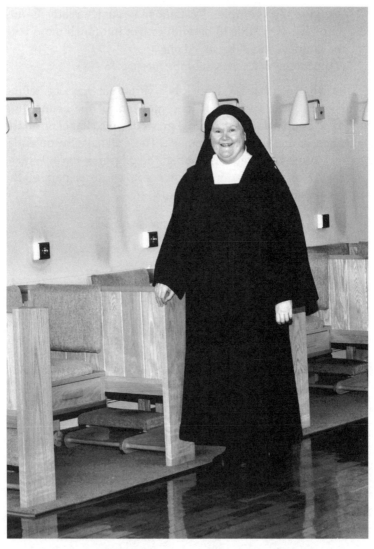

Sister Teresita, Tranquilla, Knock Carmelite Monastery

CHAPTER SEVEN

Tranquilla, Knock Carmelite Monastery: The Journey from Dublin to Knock

Sr Teresita

Those who join the Carmelite Order are not lost
to their near and dear ones, but have been won for them,
because it is our vocation to intercede to God for everyone.
Edith Stein

Edith Stein (St Teresa Benedicta of the Cross): She was born into an
orthodox Jewish family. After much searching she became a Catholic,
then became a Carmelite nun and was killed in the gas chambers at
Auschwitz in 1941.

The longest journey starts with the first step. However, if the first step is taken eastwards when the final destination (as yet unknown) is westwards, the journey takes a little longer.

Our Carmelite community arrived in Knock in October 1981. Although much work still needed to be done on our new home in the West it was wonderful to be here at last.

Our community was founded in Dolphin's Barn, Dublin in 1833, forty-seven years before the Knock apparition was to take place. In 1844, due to lack of space, the community moved to Rathmines. Sr Teresa Walsh, sister to the then Archbishop of Tuam, was among the first of our sisters. Little did she know that her bones would find their last resting place in her brother's archdiocese when we transferred our departed to a new cemetery on our grounds in Knock.

The story of our move to Knock began in the late 1970s when the oldest part of our monastery in Rathmines became a health and safety nightmare. With water running down electric wires and walls bulging to near collapse, it was clear that something had to be done. However, it was far from clear what that 'something' was. We started with the idea of building a new wing but lack of funds would not allow it. We thought of selling part of our land and then building but that proved impracticable. The only way forward seemed to be to find a new site in Dublin, sell our land and build a new monastery.

The Prioress at the time put her considerable business skills to work and, after many trials of one sort or another, we had a buyer for Rathmines. The Carmelite Friars of the Ancient Observance in Gort Muire, Ballinteer, Co Dublin – (south east of our monastery) – were kindly going to sell us a part of their land to build on. Sr Fidelma had planned it so well that the signing over of our Rathmines home to the buyer and the buying of the land in Gort Muire were to be done on the same day.

The Lord had other ideas. The night before the 'selling and buying' we got a phone call from the first Irishman to be elected General Superior of our Order, Fr Finian Monahan OCD, who was in London at the time. He had a proposition he wanted to put to us but would rather do so in person and not over the phone. He said we could sell Rathmines as planned but, to hold off buying land until he could speak to us. We began to get some idea of how Abraham must have felt.

Fr Finian arrived within a few days and pointed out that there were many other Carmelite monasteries in Dublin and would we not think of moving outside of the city. Well, we hadn't but were now called upon to try to think outside of our comfort zone. He suggested that as 'Carmel was all Mary's' and as Lourdes and Fatima had Carmels close to them, we might think of moving to Knock, home of the National Marian Shrine.

The now infamous words were uttered by our Galway Sister: 'That boggy old place?' Not the best of starts. We now put all our energy into seeing if this was where God was leading us. Archbishop Cunnane gave us permission to consult Msgr James Horan, who later freely admitted he had met his match in business in our Sr Fidelma – no small accolade! It was a call of faith to our community, especially the elders among us.

It was a disappointment to leave our plans for Gort Muire and the wonderful friends we had made with the community there. The call to 'go West' in faith to *Cnoc Mhuire* asked much of us, but through it we experienced the blessings 'pressed down and running over' promised to all who journey in faith. The warm welcome to the West was balm to our souls and we rejoice, daily, to be 'home' here in Knock.

Carmelites were, however, present in our area long before we came. The Order was founded on Mt Carmel in the Holy Land towards the end of the twelfth century. By 1240 the growing Muslim control of the Holy Land led the first 'Brothers of Our Lady of Mt Carmel' to move to Europe. A Carmelite monastery was founded, a few miles down the road from us, in Ballinasmall in 1288. It was destroyed during Penal times but a Carmelite presence was kept in the area until about 1870. A silver chalice and candlestick were kept safe and we had the joy of using them during the consecration of our small Carmelite chapel in 1981.

In our Carmelite tradition we look to Mary as Mother and Sister. Our apostolate as contemplative nuns is a silent one and the silence of the Knock apparition appeals to us in a special way. Although Knock is Ireland's National Marian Shrine, the tableau of the apparition centres more on the Lamb and the Cross – symbols of the Eucharist – than on the other figures, and has a complex theological composition that it would be hard for fifteen people to just 'make up'.

Whatever one's view on apparitions, the invitation to contemplate the Knock apparition comes without any spoken message, leaving one free to ponder it in silence. It is a tableau that our Carmelite sister, St Teresa Benedicta of the Cross (Edith Stein), would treasure. She died in Auschwitz during the Second World War but her words echo still in our day. 'The Cross is again raised before us. It is the sign of contradiction – (but) the fountain from the heart of the Lamb has not dried up – let us draw from the springs of salvation for the entire parched world.'

Prayer in Carmel is never self-centred. Since coming to Knock we have carried the words that Archbishop Cunnane spoke to us: 'To have compassion for all God's people foremost in our hearts. Many make their way up to our door, or write, to ask prayers for their various intentions. We encounter many people who entrust us with their sorrows and their joys. It is a privilege for us to become one with them as, with Mary, we look to the Lord for the healing and hope needed by our "entire parched world".'

Our Carmelite life is a simple one. 'What do you do all day?' is a common question not so easily answered. The daily community celebration of the Eucharist, the recitation of the Divine Office in common, two hours of silent, personal prayer, *Lectio Divina* (prayerful spiritual reading) and joyful recreation together, form the nucleus around which our days are built. This means work, community life and solitude blending and forming part of the whole which gives Carmel its unique identity and mission in the church.

Prayer is our main 'work' but, like everyone else, we need to earn a living. We are delighted to be able to supply the altar breads used during Mass to the shrine and other parishes. That the 'work of our human hands' will become the Bread of Life for so many makes all the labour involved worthwhile.

Although not involved in an active way in the work of the shrine we feel very much part of the parish of Knock. We owe so much to the wonderful people who have supported us in so many ways down the years. Their names are etched on our hearts and no words can express our gratitude to the priests and people (past and present), who make up the 'family' of Knock parish and shrine.

The silent apparition of Mary and the Lamb, with St Joseph and St John, continue to form us in love and we are blessed to have four sisters in formation at present. They, please God, will help carry our community into the future. We have never regretted our 'Call to the West' and we continue to sing Mary's song of joy, daily, in the Prayer of the Church, in union with all who touch and enrich our lives with their faith and trust.

Fiona McCarthy, Director of Counselling, Knock Shrine

CHAPTER EIGHT

Counselling at Knock

Fiona Mc Carthy

*If you allow yourself to be the person you are
then everything will come into rhythm.*
John O'Donohue

Knock shrine runs a Counselling Service. It is for any adult who is ex-periencing any emotional or psychological distress. Ms Fiona Mc Carthy is the Director of Counselling. She explains the work of the Counselling Service

There are many reasons why people would come to counselling. Feelings of depression, loss of interest in life, anxiety, loneliness, difficulty in relationships, low self-esteem, life just not making sense, life not being manageable. Often people will come and say 'I just don't feel right.'

In counselling people are encouraged to address these issues that are causing problems. The hope is that eventually change will occur for them. Relief that will bring about a better quality of life.

We know it is always better to speak about what we feel is going wrong for us. One time people would only speak about what happened to them in the past. We were inclined to just say it and maybe do no more about it. The saying of it was good but the saying of it in a professional setting is better. People are more open now.

The start of a counselling session is meant to give a person time to settle down. It also gives me the chance to talk about what we might call the limitations and boundaries to this process. What my role is. I'm dependent on you telling me what you want to tell me. I don't delve. Unless you are ready to give me whatever it is you want to, then it is of no value to me.

Your comfort in sharing information is as important as the

information you share. I'm trying to see your world from what you are saying to me. I'm not judging. I'm not solving but I am hoping that we will create change together.

My job is to create a relationship that helps you think about your issues. Hopefully that will encourage you to think maybe there are different ways of dealing with those issues. To think 'Maybe how I've been handling things for the last twenty years isn't really what I want.'

As we go through life we will always face difficult issues but in counselling we may learn different ways of coping. The next time it will take less time to get back up again. We work with the belief that if you don't feel happy now you have the resources to live a better life.

It might be long term. A counsellor can never tell you what your life could be but you yourself through counselling can get to a place where you can make more empowered decisions. Say you are in an abusive marriage. If you come to counselling and you are in a difficult situation and you are willing to take part in that relationship with the counsellor and you are willing to examine your situation deeply enough, movement will take place.

Child abuse: when we first meet someone who comes for counselling in this area I give the usual overview of what counselling is and isn't about. But in the case of child abuse I need to go further. If I believe from what you tell me there is somebody else at risk I will say to you that you should call to your social worker and report that. If you feel you can't do that there may be situations I will feel I have to do what you don't want me to do.

I know our priorities are clients but I must say those things at the beginning. Otherwise I will lull you into a false sense of believing confidentiality is limitless, which is not the case.

The recession has created problems for people. Loss of jobs. Loss of income. Loss of independence and identity. All these create desperate situations for an awful lot of people. Clearly in counselling we cannot create jobs but we can facilitate people to come back from the brink.

The three biggest issues for people? Relationships, depression and low self-esteem.

We provide two services here. One is the kind I have been

describing. We have a number of fully trained counsellors who offer short and long term work.

Then we have single listening sessions, with volunteers who have counselling skills. It isn't counselling as such but it's an important service because it facilitates people who may not necessarily want or need counselling. It is very immediate. You can do what the name says – drop in. We have people here available. Naturally there will be times when we won't have someone available immediately to talk to. People understand that.

What we are finding from people who 'drop in' is that they often find the first contact so useful that they often go a step further and go into counselling itself.

Mike Byrne, Journalist and Broadcaster

CHAPTER NINE

Knock and My Story

Mike Byrne

*It doesn't really matter if Our Lady appeared at Knock
as long as it is now a place where you can be honest
about the frailty of your life.*

I live in Ballyhaunis a few miles from Knock. I was brought up
in a pub and shop. An old fashioned pub. A man's pub.

Knock really didn't mean much to me as a young fellow.
During the summer months and in August during the big novena
we'd have a lot of strangers coming into the shop and into the
pub on their way to and from Knock. Knock was business.

When the pope came to Knock in 1979 Ballyhaunis was black
with security. I was in my early twenties and to be honest Knock
was a place out the road where a lot of people went. It meant very
little to me. I knew they said Our Lady appeared there but that was
it.

As a young fellow I used to wonder did it ever happen at all.
I did. My father used often say it was all made up. He put it
down to drink. Even though he drove my mother out there
every Thursday.

There's no knowing the Irish Catholic mind.

Thursday was a closed day in Ballyhaunis . They'd spend the
day out there in Knock. And any vigil in Knock, my mother
would go. I used to say wasn't she the daft thing to be out there
praying until four in the morning. What was she doing?
'Praying for you' was the answer. That meant nothing to me
then. It does now.

I went to church on Sunday. That's what we did back then. I
suppose I always had a faith hidden in the heart but it was covered with so much stuff – football, girls, everything and anything. Whatever faith was there was well buried at the bottom of
the rubble.

Anyway, I ran the pub for twenty-five years. And then in

1997 I was diagnosed with MS . It got so bad my wife and myself decided to get out of the pub. I was suffering physically and from depression. With the depression I had no interest in chatting. If you can't talk running a pub you might as well get out of it. Your main tool in a pub is the tongue. You have to be able to keep your end up in the crack. I couldn't.

I was asked would I go to Medjugorje. I went totally against my will. I was suffering too much.

I came back cured. As simple as that. The depression that crucified me for three years was gone. The MS was gone. The neurologist I was going to had intended starting me on a course of treatment. There was no need now. The thing is I didn't go to be cured. I had gone against my will.

Strangest of all when I came home I felt more than my body was cured. I felt a change in how I saw things. Things that mattered up to that just meant little to me now.

I was home. Mudjugorje was over there. But Knock was next door. So I started going to Knock. Remember, Knock was the place people went to and if we were lucky they came into our shop or pub on the way.

Now it was different. I now was one of those people, a pilgrim and full of gratitude for my health. Before being dragged to Medjugorje I hadn't wanted to get out of bed or open the curtains. Now I wanted to be with people. I went for Knock hook line and sinker.

I found a meaning in Mass in Knock. Either in the old church or in the Apparition Chapel. The apparition site was special to me because one of the visionaries was a Dominick Byrne. His brother was a great grandfather of mine. That hadn't meant much to me. Now it did.

I was sitting in the Apparition Chapel one day. Just thinking and praying and it struck me everyone coming into the chapel, everyone I saw on the grounds, was broken. Something in life was crucifying them. That was what we all had in common. That was what we all had in common with Mary. With that Knock clicked into place.

Knock was about healing. Mary was about healing. The Masses, the silent and spoken prayers the Reconciliation Chapel, the meeting with total strangers others and the telling of our stories and troubles to each other – Knock is one big beautiful place of healing.

So now? I thank Our Lady every day for where I am now in life's journey. Some say some of us have a devotion to Mary that somehow blocks out Jesus. But look at the *Magnificat*. 'My soul glorifies the Lord.' Mary said that. We go to Jesus through Mary. I have come to a love of Jesus and his teaching about life through devotion to Mary.

What would I say to someone who says it is all daft, all make believe to help people like me cope?

No. The fifteen visionaries were all ages up to x years of age. How would you get x number of Irish people with that age span to agree on a concocted story?

Strange thing. It doesn't really matter if Our Lady appeared at Knock as long as it is now a place where you can be honest about the frailty of your life. It doesn't matter because Mary is bringing people to a place where they are being brought back to spiritual, mental health. And brought back to Jesus.

The time I'm at Knock gives me perspective. Before I was selfish, self-centred. The world revolved around me. I set standards for others I didn't set for myself. I looked down on people who didn't match up to my ideas of how they should be. Not, of course, that I set high standards for myself.

Now? Going to Knock as often as I do has modified my attitudes. I get more time to reflect, to pray about my attitudes and outlook. Now I look at people completely differently. I put myself out for people more. It's been gradual and I put the change down to the time spent at Knock. Reflecting, praying. Just being there.

It has given me massive peace. It's the return visits that do it. Mass there each day. Prayers every day. The sacrament of Reconciliation every month. All these open the heart.

Monica Morley, Director of the Family Life and Prayer Centre,
Knock Shrine

CHAPTER TEN

The Family Life & Prayer Centre
Monica Morley

*If religion means anything it is about people
and people by and large live out their lives in family networks.*

Since the shrine at Knock established itself as a central place of pilgrimage, the Family Life & Prayer Centre has been at the heart of it. Founded to support and enrich families, its ministry has grown and developed over the years. Its mission remains the same – to acknowledge the role that families play in shaping our parishes, our society and our country.

Knowing as we do how significant early childhood experiences are in all of this, the focus on resourcing and supporting the family unit and nurturing it within a faith context is what drives the work of the Family Life and Prayer Centre. For some people family experiences, due to a variety of reasons – death, separation, rejection etc – can be difficult. That, too, is part of the mix of the ministry.

Monica Morley is Director of the Family Life and Prayer Centre in Knock. She explains its work in more detail.

A pilgrimage to Knock operates at two levels. You have this huge group of people all seemingly doing the same thing, but within that community you have a whole lot of individuals each with their own individuality and needs.

Something about Knock helps us step aside from the crowd, go into our own world, attend to what bothers us and yet not lose the sense of being with others. That is the richness of Knock.

For over thirty years the Family Life Centre at Knock has been about meeting people in that space where they find themselves alone with their worries. The challenge is what we can do for them.

The Family Life Centre is there to help us deal with what could broadly be called life-changing experiences. For example, going from being single to being married. Suddenly you have to work out what it means to be in this different situation. You find it can be a source of happiness or not. You can be stopped in your tracks when you realise the dream may not become a reality.

Many people may think the biggest problems are about sex but what you find is that more often than not money is the problem.

We may start off with clear ideas about what is my money and what is your money but then we find it is about shared money and for some that asks for major adjustments. The money thing is really a symbol of my identity and sense of control versus your identity and sense of control. My life versus your life.

You try to get behind the money problem to the problem that underlies it. My sense of who I am if I either have or haven't money. What is this tension over money saying about my own sense of who I am, my sense of sharing, my security in myself? The thing is, if I have security in myself the money won't be an issue.

This problem has changed hugely since the early days of the Family Life Centre. Back then, thirty years ago, men were mainly the wage earners and involved more in permanent work. Women accepted that role much easier.

That has changed and the change has created more problems for men than women. That can lead to marriage breakdown but more seriously to emotional breakdown, which can range from mild to severe.

The Knock Family Centre provides counselling and awareness in these situations. We network with the Family Centre in Castlebar and elsewhere.

It goes without saying that over the years the whole notion of family has changed. So we have had to change our vision of what the Family Life Centre is about. In the early years the definition of family was very tradition and very defined. Take the traditional Catholic attitudes towards birth control and abortion. In Family Life we certainly put out these positions but we don't make them a make or break issue in our contact with people.

Our religion is important in our own lives and it automatically comes out in our work. Again we've had to change ourselves. A lot of our own certainties and views have had to be modified. As you get older you change and your certainties change. That has happened myself and inevitably it has changed the way I deal with people.

Why a service like this in Knock? If religion means anything it is about people and people by and large live out their lives in family networks. So it is natural that Knock has this focus on family.

I find there is something very different about people who have a personal experience of brokenness. People who have reflected on it and now, with the advantage of a bit of distance from the experience, have integrated it. These people who know what a broken heart is have something to offer you never can offer without that experience.

There is a richness that comes from brokenness. An acceptance that we are certain of very little. A tolerance of diversity. An appreciation of the mystery of it all. A kind of rawness that makes you appreciate other people in a way you cannot otherwise.

That is one of two things I have learnt from working at Knock. The other is the openness and wisdom of people who have lived a long life.

Older people come into the Rest and Care Centre here in Knock several days a week. Meeting one old man who comes in is about the best part of my week. Listening to him talk is like seeing life through a long lens. It has depth, width, and wisdom.

These older people are aware of the fragility of life. Of how short the whole thing is. We sometimes call their faith 'simple faith'. Far from it. It is not simple but faith born of simplicity – something totally different. The simplicity of someone who has tried and tested life, has been tried and tested by life and has now distilled it down to what's important and what isn't.

One important part of the work of the Family Life Centre grew out of a personal experience.

My sister's boyfriend died. They were engaged. After his death his and our own parents used to meet in our house. From them I got a real sense of the nightmare this was. Out of that I thought maybe there are others going through the same agonies. Maybe we need something in Knock.

The six meetings in our house became twelve. Then as more

and more started to come we moved to a larger room in Knock. Then a hall and then a bigger hall and finally to the Rest and Care Centre.

What this says to me is that there is a rawness in life and when I am touched by it I have a need to cling to other people who in some sense have the same faith perspective as myself. In reality I am clinging on to my own life, my despair is so great. There is terror in the lack of hope and fear I cannot live on.

Now we provide a place, a sacred space, in Knock where people can feel they are with people who 'have gone through what I have gone through. People who know I'm not crazy. I can talk about how I feel.'

Even though our bereavement work is in the faith context it is also very much focused on the terrible human hurt that is in the death of someone we love. It is saying this is a dreadful human experience. This is the challenge of constantly keeping Knock serving both the faith and human experiences of pilgrims.

On Bereavement Sunday we try to respect that dual dimension of bereavement. Firstly, the human experience of loss. And secondly, what our faith says about the larger context of our lives and the few years we are here. Those two readings of life are an important backdrop to the day for the 600 or so who gather in the Rest and Care Centre. People meet, talk, listen. Share a common burden.

We have Mass on the day. Very little is said at the Mass because very little needs to be said. The Eucharist in itself is healing. At it most effective it touches hearts, gives a sense of burdens being lightened and hopefully a hint of sorrows being understood in the bigger scale of things.

After Mass there is tea, refreshments and friendship. People meet, talk, listen. Share common burdens. They come from all over the country. For some this is the only time they meet each other and they are slow to part.

I am involved in a Sunday morning religious programme on Mid West, the local radio station. In ways it is an extension of the weekday work at the shrine.

In recent years both the shrine and the radio raise the same questions. Why are we not reaching our full potential as a

church and as a shrine? We know we should be constantly push-
ing ourselves outside our comfort zone. We fail to be honest
about reality.

Take the gap between the spiritual hunger in people and
what the church offers to satisfy that hunger. It is very painful to
recognise that so many young people are walking away. It's a
reality at family level, at parish level, at diocesan level. But we
don't seem to want to take on board that reality. We seem to feel
we don't need to panic just yet. Sure, the numbers are down and
dropping but we're okay yet. Maybe the recession will bring
them back.

I'm talking about the group 20-40. The young mothers and
fathers. Their yoga, reflexology, anything alternative, at the very
least indicate a spiritual curiosity. But our worlds don't meet.
We seem uncomfortable with them even though we know from
our own nephews and nieces they are just youngsters finding
their way.

John O'Donohue had this picture of young people moving
around among food stalls. There we are with our beautiful gran-
ary of richness. We ourselves believe in what we have to offer
but we are doing no business. There is some mismatch between
the hunger of the young and what they perceive we have to
give.

It is only at times like Christmas morning that you realise
what it would mean if they were helped feel they belong.

Sister Mary Hernon, Knock Prayer Guidance Centre

CHAPTER ELEVEN

The Knock Prayer Guidance Centre
Sr Mary Hernan

Sacred scripture isn't merely a text written in the past,
but rather the word of God that has within it
a personal message directed to each individual Christian.
Pope Benedict

There is a growing recognition that we starve our faith when we are casual about the relevance of scripture in our lives. Part of Knock's response is The Prayer Guidance Centre . It is there to help pilgrims appreciate and pray scripture. Sr Mary Hernan is a Mercy Sister and works with the Centre.

I taught in Mary Immaculate Training College in Limerick. At one stage I set up a prayer group with the students. It focused on praying the scriptures. While it helped that the students were already studying scripture it is important to say anyone can come raw to a scripture prayer group and benefit from it. I felt as did the students that the prayer group was opening some useful channel of spirituality that we mostly ignore.

Around that time I did a thirty-day retreat. It was just what I needed. I was always attracted to what we call the contemplative life. This retreat helped me to have more courage and seriously see if that way of life was for me.

Some time later I went on a pilgrimage to the Holy Land. One day we came to Bethsaida. That's where Jesus met the man who had spent thirty-eight years sitting by the healing pool waiting for someone to help him get in (John 5). Jesus said to him: 'Get up. Pick up your pack and walk.'

The man had been complaining that no one was helping him get into the pool and change his life. So he just sat there for thirty-eight years. Moaning and blaming everyone else. Not letting go of his fear.

That was both his story and mine. I was learning two things. One was that scripture has two meanings. One for the people who first lived the incident. The second meaning was for the person now meditating on it. For that man the lesson was to let go of his fears. For me the lesson was to follow my gut feeling.

Another day we came to Mount Tabor (Mk 9:1-8). This was the scene of the transfiguration where Jesus showed his close friends who he was and what his mission in life was. His friends weren't too sure what he meant.

Again we have the two levels in scripture. The story as lived then on that mountain. The story as lived now by me. My best and closest friends weren't too sure either what I was about.

I came home and took spiritual direction. That's a conversation about life in the light of faith. Where you meet and talk with a more spiritually experienced person about the ways God may be touching your life.

Spiritual direction is as old as scripture. It is what Jesus did in the gospels. His conversations with Nicodemus, with the woman at the well, with Peter and the other apostles.

In spiritual direction today you try to tease out with your spiritual director, in a prayerful way, what direction your life might take. The director (trained in discernment) listens. He or she feeds back what he or she has heard. No judgement. That prayerful talking and listening can go over several sessions. With prayer and guidance you hope to reach a point where you know what to do. I reached that point. I came to Knock.

We have a beautiful centre here. A lot of thought has gone into the atmosphere a pilgrim meets from the moment he or she comes in the front door.

We start with a quiet time. Most people have just come in off the grounds and need a chance to relax, settle and come to a still-ness. To try to gently become aware of God's presence.

Each session is led by a Prayer Guide. We have over a hund - red guides, each trained in prayer guidance and spiritual direc-tion. These Prayer Guides are from all over Ireland and England. They work in teams of four a week over the 24/25 week pilgrim-age season. There is regular updating of training and continu-ous review of how to provide the best possible service to the people who come to The Prayer Guidance Centre.

This is what happens at a Prayer Guidance session. There is a time to settle and be at ease within yourself. The prayer space is carefully planned to create this atmosphere. In time a passage of scripture is read. Then we have a quiet time where we each look at the two levels of scripture. What it meant back when it first happened. Secondly what it might be saying to each of present in our own situation.

No one has to share unless they want to. No one need feel out of it if they don't know much scripture. It is not class.

The session lasts 30 minutes. Just talking about it like this makes it seem so ordinary but it really can change lives.

Some examples of that. I remember one day we took the story of the agony in the garden. The people left when the session was over. One woman came back. She shared that reflecting on the story was the first time she was able to grieve the loss of her husband two years before.

Another day I took that section from Isaiah 43 where one of the lines says: you are precious in my eyes and I love you. Afterwards this grown man, he could be seventy years of age, came up to me and tears rolling down his face. He reached out his hand, shook mine and said 'Thank you.' It came to me that this might have been the first time in his life this man heard he was loved.

Another time a woman and her husband were in the group. She had a worry from the past. We had prayed over Isaiah 3:18-19. 'No need to recall the past, or dwell on what happened long ago. See I am doing a new deed. Can you not see it?'

During the meditation time the worry had come back to the wife. The husband sensed this. He was standing with her and said quietly: 'Don't you remember the lines we prayed about? No need to recall the past?' Her face just lit up as he reminded her of the quote. I felt what a beautiful relationship is there.

All kinds of people either come for one of the sessions or just drop in for quiet time between sessions. Some are Christians of other denominations. One Friday a Jewish rabbi dropped in. We were reflecting on Psalm 46:10, 'Be still and know that I am God.' The rabbi stayed for the whole session. As he was leaving he told us that we had given him just what he needed at that moment. He was thrilled he stayed. Even though as a Jew, he should be already in Belfast to prepare for the start of the Sabbath. This and other stories like it give us hope.

Mary Neary, Chief Handmaid, Knock Shrine

CHAPTER TWELVE

The Knock Shrine Handmaids
Mary Neary
tells of her travels to find her place and vocation in Knock.
She is the Chief Handmaid at the Shrine

Two roads diverged in a wood,
and I took the one less travelled by,
and that has made all the difference.
Robert Frost

Knock Shrine Society of Handmaids and Stewards, founded in 1935, is
a voluntary body and its members are committed to serving the church
at Knock. This work has continued for the past 76 years. Members
come from all over Ireland, from all walks of life and from all age
groups. Those who are 18 years of age and not more than 55 can apply
to become registered members. You can contact the main Knock Shrine
office. New handmaids must write a detailed letter about themselves to
the Honorary Secretary. Those under 18 years of age can join the
Youth Section.

The handmaids are involved in the ceremonies in Knock. They act
as Ministers of the Eucharist and assist the sick, elderly and those with
special needs. The handmaids also take care of catering for both the
helpers and the sick. Some of them carry out office duties and work in
the Souvenir Shop.

I was born in Belmullet, Co Mayo. I grew up with devotion to
Mary: the rosary at night, holy pictures in the house. I left for the
US at eighteen and settled in Philadelphia. I was young and at
one stage thought I was on the way to be married and have a
family. That didn't work out. I came back to Ireland and then
went to England. My mother got a stroke. So I came back from
England to mind her.

All through my time in Philadelphia and England I had a
strong devotion to Mary. If I had got married I think that a
strong prayer life would still have been important to me. I had

been reared to see Mary as a mother always there to help. I would have believed that to be true in any walk of life.

When I was home in Belmullet I went on pilgrimage to Knock with my parents. I happened to see a copy of the *Knock Shrine Annual*. It was there I saw a piece welcoming the Carmelite sisters to Knock. They were contemplatives. For some reason that stirred feelings that what I really wanted was a life where prayer and silence were important. A religious way of life had always drawn me. But as I said I had met someone in the US. That had put everything on hold for a while. But now I read the news that the Carmelites had picked Knock where they could follow their way of living their vocation. I felt maybe Knock was where I could too.

My mother died in 1980. I came to Knock and started to work as handmaid in St Joseph's in the shrine grounds. St Joseph's is where disabled people come for a break during the pilgrimage season.

I had found my place. The end of the line in my search. The prayer, the work, the people I worked with, the whole atmosphere. The mix of hectic busyness and quiet prayer times during the pilgrimage season. The quiet and silence during the off season.

The patients taught me patience. Beautiful people. Parents who had led active, independent lives now in wheelchairs, waiting to get someone to bring them to the toilet, someone to help wash and feed them. I had never seen a person in a wheelchair until I saw my mother in one. Now much of my life is spent with people like her. It is seven days a week work but it was what I needed.

Some of them had questions about the goodness of God. Some hadn't prayed much in their lives and were clear when they came to St Joseph that this prayer life wasn't for them.

But they did go along with the prayer routine. Mass at ten, Eucharistic adoration and rosary until twelve. Lunch. Then a rest or Mass at the shrine. Then the shops. And finally the anointing of the sick. A full day.

My time with the disabled helped me a lot. It deepened my faith. Something about the mix of prayer and service of others seemed right. So much so I became what we call a Dedicated

Handmaid. People living in the world but with the vows of poverty, obedience and chastity.

Our handmaids come from all over the country. Mothers, grannies who have had good lives, loving husbands, children. Women who want to give something back.

A wish for pilgrims? That Knock would help them appreciate the sacraments. Especially Mass and the sacrament of Reconciliation.

As for myself, I am happy I did what I did with my life. All the bits and pieces – home, Philadelphia , England – have led to this.

Helen Toner, Youth Ministry Director, Knock Shrine

CHAPTER THIRTEEN

Youth Ministry at Knock
Helen Toner

*'What is clear is that there is a disconnect between them
(young people) and the institutional church. They believe in God.
They don't believe in the church. It is not hostility.
Just that it is not in their world.'*

When people think of Knock shrine they naturally think of the older generations, but the late Msgr Joe Quinn felt there was a real need for something for younger people.

So what we do is a day programme for the students. A teacher will get in touch with us and we look for a bit of information on the students. The age, what year they are in and so on. Then we do up a programme for them.

I know there is an impression that young people aren't interested in religion. That could be true but what it may mean is that they are not necessarily interested in what we might call the practice of religion in normal parish life. But when they come to us for day they are interested.

They come in and you can see they are under tremendous pressure. Some of that pressure comes from society at the minute. Take the media. You have to look a certain way, you have to have certain things, be always busy. You really don't have a minute. And the odd minute they just might be free they are listening to their I-pod or sending a text or on facebook.

What we say to them is that I don't think all these thing are a waste of time – technology now is brilliant and we can get so much out of these new things – but we ask them to think what happens when something goes wrong; when something happens in their families or someone hurts them. Just then are all these things we spend time on enough or do we need more?

I try to tell them God is in everything, in the good and the bad and that he is there through it all.

A huge thing in the retreat is that they are very aware of family problems. At the start I ask for a show of hands on who has the perfect family at home. No one will ever put up their hand.

I ask them what does that mean and they say 'But no one is perfect.' And you can see that answer says what is in their minds. The fact no hand went up tells each of them maybe our set-up at home isn't perfect but it's alright.

I ask who would share their family problems and no hands go up. They don't want people to judge their families; don't want the peer pressure from others knowing about their families.

They feel they constantly have to wear a mask. They might have to wear a mask in school in front of their friends but when they get home they have to wear one as well . The mask is saying that in school and at home everything is perfect. Everything is fine.

We try to get behind that. We say just talk to God in a letter. In that letter you can say whatever you want in the knowledge that nobody looks at the letters. We don't look at them. Nobody does. That's the promise.

We say this is your chance to get all that stuff out of the way. Maybe you have never told anybody these things ever. Just write them down. When you are done fold them and put them away.

When they are finished we ask what they think. Usually they say that at the start we didn't think we had much to say but once you get the first line out you realise you have loads to say.

The point of this is that it will open up the process of prayer. A lot of them when they think of prayer they think only of Hail Marys or the church .What we are trying to say is that this is a different way of praying. A way of being at home with God and getting everything out there. This is the self-reflective part of the day.

Then we sit and do a quiet meditation where I ask the kids to hand that letter over to Jesus and ask him to take care of it.

I say 'Suppose you write a letter to God and you say "my parents are always fighting and I think they are going to get a divorce".' I say writing this doesn't mean when I go home mam and dad are back together again and that they will never, ever fight again – that God has fixed it that way.

But what you might get from that prayer is that God might help you yourself handle how this is affecting you or that God will help them in their relationship.

In another part of the retreat we have a thing called Question Box and in that we ask them some general questions. They can say what they want. They write their answers on a piece of paper and fold them and put them in the box. Afterwards we read them out.

One question is 'What does God mean to me?' Nearly all say 'God means a lot to me.' 'God is someone I can talk to.' 'I feel God listens to me.' As you see, all positive answers.

What is clear is that there is a disconnect between them and the institutional church. They believe in God. They don't believe in the church. If I were to say we'll have Mass now there would be a groan from those young people who were just after writing such positive things about the place of God in their lives.

At this stage Nicola Flaherty, who works here with me, tries to explain the Mass and what it is about.

The image of church is that it has too many rules and regul - ations. It isn't in the real world. It is disconnected from what they are going through. This isn't hostility. Just that it is not in their world. If you asked would it make a difference if the priest was cool and the choir great you'd get a big 'Yes' because that connects with their world. It is difficult to see how this problem of the image of the church is going to be handled but it has to be.

The next part of the day is out and about. A tour of the shrine area. You'd be surprised at how many of the young people don't know a thing about the apparition. When we get to the Appar - ition Chapel and hear the story, many of them find the whole idea strange.

And yet at the very end of the day when we bring them into the Apparition Chapel for ten minutes silence they love it.

We go to the museum on our tour. They really get interested in how people dressed and lived the time of the apparition.

Next stop is the Cenacolo. This is a community living in a house in Knock parish. They are addicts aged 18-30. Their rehabilitation is built on spirituality, not medication.

We bring only the more senior student to the Cenacolo. The stories they hear are very real to the young people. The are not

of the style of 'I was in the gutter and all of a sudden God appeared to me and I saw the light.' Nothing sensational. Just addicts who want a life.

Many of the young people living in the Cenacolo never
prayed the rosary before. Now they do. Few sat in front of the
Blessed Sacrament. Now they do every day of their recovery.
Part of that recovery is to recognise the hurt they caused their
families and those who loved them. They pray for God's help in
this difficult part of their lives.

It is a difficult regime but the young students we bring there
discover that those in the community have a great peace.

We come back to The Youth Centre and get ready for a
Reconciliation Service. It includes he sacrament of Reconciliation for those who wish. We hope we are coming at Confession
a different way. That it is not something we do for God but
something he does to us. It is about coming back, reconnecting
with God.

This helps. Suppose I say Jesus is in the next room and you
can go in and tell him everything you have done. How many
would go? All hands up. But if I say we are going to have
Confession today, about two hands would go up.

Maybe what make us that way is that we go in saying the
same three things we've been saying ever since our First
Communion. Or maybe making up things we never did. Of
course you get nothing out of that kind of confession. So the
challenge is to go in and make a proper confession. They will
and they do.

The day ends with some time before the Blessed Sacrament.
They simply love it. Even young people who may have been
lively during the day settle down to this. You could hear a pin
drop.

How much of this could be done at parish level? I think all of
it. 100%. They need to connect with parish. I don't think that's
happening. A lot of kids in secondary schools never see the
priest. He's an alien to them. That's worrying because if they see
the priest not connecting with them the church becomes more
alien. I think that is why students more and more are saying 'I
like saying my own prayers.'

For myself I suppose I started on the road to this work from a personal experience on a school retreat. Then I went to college to do theology to learn more. Growing up I said the usual prayers but there was no connection with my life. The priest at the retreat spoke about that. If it doesn't mean anything to you what are you at? When you talk to God you have to be open and honest. Tell him everything about what is going on in you. From that I developed the habit of talking to God.

I knew I wanted to get into youth ministry. But at the same time I never felt part of parish. A friend sent me the ad for the job here in Knock. I answered and here I am. Not as holy as I should be.

I came to the Summer Festival at Knock. I went to confession and I told the poor priest everything including that I was taking this job but I was terrified. He said God wasn't stupid and he wouldn't have me do something I'm not able for. I got great comfort from that. And it was only when I started here the first year that I realised what God's love had planned for me.

What I've learnt about being a Christian is that it is important to see God in the everyday. The uniqueness of each of us. Also that we need to share faith with others. There is nothing like standing with a hundred others saying the same prayer. Also sharing with others that moment after receiving the Eucharist. Complete silence. That is so important.

I'd say this to priests: 'Don't be afraid of young people. Don't be intimidated.' We all have to push ourselves outside our comfort zone. With everything that is happening now, priests are shy of going into school but face the issues and talk about them. Show that you are human. Young people are in tune with that.

Carmel Neary, Manager, Knock Shrine Bookshop

CHAPTER FOURTEEN

Knock Shrine Bookshop

Carmel Neary, Manager

In recent times pilgrims and tourists visiting Knock Shrine purchase a great number of religious books. Apart from priests and religious, many lay people appear to be good readers of publications that they have heard of or seen advertised. Teachers who come to the shrine with groups of students also find publications they need in the Knock bookshop. They are always looking for resource books for help in their work.

The Knock Shrine Website,www.knock-shrine.ie, gives them easy to read information about our books and the thousands who come to Knock can, of course, experience the shrine bookshop for themselves.

Provision of religious books is a very worthwhile service and an appropriate Apostolate for a national Marian Shrine.

The Categories of books that are constant sellers and always in demand in huge numbers are, in the order of importance, books on faith, eucharistic adoration, spirituality, prayer and meditation; devotional books, mariology including Knock Shrine literature; books on scripture, bibles, and homiletics. Nowadays, people are anxious to deepen their knowledge of the faith and are educating themselves by reading good authors. They are seeking answers to various important questions and this has to be beneficial both for themselves and for the church.

Scripture is very popular because they realise that it will be more centre-stage from now on. Many find that *Lectio Divina,* so popular for centuries, is now 'in' again and is a valuable way of reading and praying the bible. Of course, Pope Benedict's Exhortation on the Word of God – *Verbum Domini* – is the most important document on sacred scripture since Vatican II.

Another very popular category with pilgrims is Eucharistic adoration as most parishes in the country now have some time devoted to it and there is a good response to it from the faithful.

The idea of providing a religious books service for pilgrims and others first came to prominence in the late Msgr James Horan's time in Knock which spanned the period from 1963 to 1986. He believed there was a need to provide such a service at the national shrine. The service began in a small way with a small book storage area at the parish church and small outlets for the books, at various points in the grounds.

His successor, Msgr Dominick Grealy served at Knock from 1986 to 2002 and he had the new religious bookshop built as he believed there was then need to expand the apostolate. Pilgrim numbers were growing all the time. It proved to be a great success as management and staff invested a great deal of hard work in the various aspects of the business.

Then in 2002, before Msgr Grealy retired, a new extension was added to the bookshop to provide more space for stock and to make for ease of movement. This new extension was opened for business in 2003 and had the support and blessing of the new Parish Priest of Knock, Msgr Joseph Quinn.

This new and elegantly furnished shop, located across from the Blessed Sacrament Chapel in theshrine grounds, is computerised, provides a Mail Order Service and is open seven days a week throughout the year.

In addition to the wide range of book categories, there are also many souvenir items stocked, many of which are specifically related to Knock, for example, the beautiful Ghirelli of Italy Rosaries and the Knock Crystal Gift Collection, shrine pictures, postcards and calendars, Knock medallions, medals and key rings. The management and staff took a special interest in this aspect of the shop and worked hard to make it a success.

A recent trend is the growth in the sales of both DVDs and CDs. Of note in the CD department is the CD of the new Knock Hymn which is entitled 'Hymn of the Apparition at Knock' which tells the story of the great event that took place here on 21 August 1879. The lyrics were composed by Tom Neary, Chief Steward of Knock and the vocal and instrumental music was composed by Sr Marie Dunne CHF, a Holy Faith nun who is well known for her musical talents and who has frequently featured on radio and television. The singer on the CD is Patricia D'Souza.

The Knock bookshop serves a number of purposes. It is part-
icularly helpful to people who have many personal problems
and difficulties. They regularly ask for books they could read
that might help them to solve their difficulties. Sometimes their
problems may have to do with family members, children or
teenagers. Widespread nowadays are problems related to drink
and drugs, break-up of marriages and relationships, financial
stress and many more. They seek solutions through reading
and, of course, through prayer. Those who are bereaved often
look for consolation in books by authors who are experts in this
field. Many people come in search of healing and find accounts
of other people's experiences to be helpful.

All kinds of people visit the Knock bookshop. While most are
ordinary Irish citizens, an increasing number now come from
countries around the world and ask for booklets that will give
them the story of Knock, as they usually do not know it prior to
their visit.

Many well known and famous people have called in over the
years, some to browse and others to make purchases. Here are
just a small number of examples: Fr Raniero Cantalamessa OFM
Cap, Preacher to the Papal Household since 1980 in the reign of
Pope John Paul II and presently in the reign of Pope Benedict
XVI, Maureen O'Hara, Sr Briege McKenna, Dana Rosemary
Scallon, Eileen Reid, Mother Teresa's Nuns, numerous church
dignitaries such as Cardinal Murphy O'Connor of Westminster,
Cardinal Seán Brady of Armagh, the Rectors of the Marian
Shrines of Europe, including Bishop Jacques Perrier of Tarbes
and Lourdes, Marion Carroll who was cured at Knock, Susan
Boyle who became famous because of her success on the TV pro-
gramme *Britain's got Talent*. Many writers and media personnel
have visited the shrine bookshop and were impressed with its
stock and its attractiveness.

People can purchase books in the Knock Shrine shop, or via
the shrine website: www.knock-shrine.ie and if they wish to
purchase souvenirs on line, they can do so via the Knock Shrine
shop in Limerick city which can also be accessed via the shrine
website. The telephone number of the Limerick shop is : (061)
419458 and the Fax number is: (061) 419458. If contacting by

post, the address is: Knock Religious Bookshop & Office, 76/77 Little Catherine Street, Limerick.

   It may be useful to know that there is a Knock Shrine Office and Religious Bookshop in England. Its address is 101, Deansgate, Manchester, M3 2BQ. The telephone number is: (0161) 8192558 and the Fax number is: (0161) 8340744. The E-mail address is: knockshrineoffice@btconnect.com.

   It is very easy to contact the Knock Shrine bookshop, in any of the following ways:

   By using the Online Shop, on the Knock Shrine website: www.knock-shrine.ie

   By Telephone: +353 (0) 94 9375030;

   By Fax: +353 (0) 94 9375031.

   By E-mail: bookshop@knock-shrine.ie

   By Post to: Knock Shrine Religious Bookcentre, Knock, Co Mayo, Ireland.

When next you visit Knock, do drop in to the shrine bookshop, at least for a browse and who can tell, you might even spot a gem of a book that you may not be able to resist. In any event – Happy Reading!

Bernie Byrne, Businessman, Knock

CHAPTER FIFTEEN

Souvenirs of Knock
Bernie Byrne

*The soul ... has many symbols
with which it reaches toward God.*
Anya Seton

*Until the pope came to Knock in 1979 the streets in Knock were lined
with stalls. As part of the preparation Msgr Horan suggested the stall
owners might like to tidy up the place. In no time the stalls were gone
and in their place rows of classy looking shops. Bernie Byrne owns one
of those shops on the Main Street.*

My grandfather, Dominck Snr, was one of the visionaries. He
died from pneumonia a few years before I was born. My father
was shy about talking about the apparition. What we learnt we
heard from aunts and uncles.

I do know my grandmother used to do bed and breakfast for
the pilgrims. The kitchen floor would be covered with stretchers
waiting to be brought up to the church. She always said she saw
many cures.

As Knock got busy with pilgrims my father opened up a souv -
enir shop and two stalls. As we sons came along and grew up
we used to ask him for a stall for ourselves. Which he gave. Even
though the stalls are over thirty years gone now and replaced by
respectable looking souvenir shops there's a woman who still
comes and asks 'Which is Bernie's stall?'

A lot has changed over the years. The increase in foreigners
is noticeable. Asians, Pakistanies, Filipinos, Chinese. All
Christians. All ages, all good buyers.

There is one picture of the Sacred Heart which is a huge buy
with them. It is as big as those mirrors you get over fireplaces.
They bring these holy pictures home by plane.

By contrast the bulk of Irish shoppers are on the elderly side. As against that there is a noticeable increase in young couples over the last two years or so. Maybe the times have something to do with but it is a nice development. We don't see teenagers.

What sells? Well, for one thing, there is much greater variety than twenty or thirty years ago. There are all the standards like the Child of Prague, rosary beads, little medals for children at home, small cameras that show religious themes and rings they bring to granddaughters.

And snow storms. You know these little souvenirs with the globe of glass and inside it a holy scene. You shake it and start a snow storm. You let the flakes settle and start again. Still as popular as ever.

Now though there is much more. Angels are, as they say, mega – angel rings, angel pens, angel key rings. This has all exploded in the last four to five years.

As have personalised souvenirs. Souvenirs that have the name of the person you are bringing the gift to. We sell a lot of personalised mementoes that families can put on graves.

The pilgrimage season has lengthened over the years. Time was it lasted from mid August to early September. Now it lasts from early April to late October. Another change is that while the weekends are busiest there is a fair sprinkling of pilgrims every day of the week.

One thing I must say. Knock to me is special. I know it is where I make a living but it means much more than that to me and my family. The fact that Dominick Snr, my grandfather, was a visionary, of course, gives me a very special closeness. If I am ever uptight the first place I go is up the grounds. That has a calming effect.

I get asked about the apparition. Do I believe in it? Yes. There is no doubt in my mind. None. Just take fifteen people in 1879. In today's terms, uneducated. How could they have come up with an apparition as complicated as the Knock apparition? As well as Mary, you have the altar, the Lamb, St John teaching from the bible, St Joseph. Too sophisticated to make up.

Any changes I'd like? So much has been done over the years I'm slow to make suggestions. Maybe the Calvary hill might be worked on. Better Stations of the Cross there. The rosary honoured in some way in that area. And maybe one addition to the services in church. To have the Anointing of the Sick at one definite Mass a fixed day of the week during the winter/off season. There are more winter pilgrims than ever before.

Knock has come a long way from my grandfather's time. From the days when my grandmother's kitchen floor was covered with pilgrims' stretchers. A long way from the hectic days removing the stalls to prepare for the pope in September 1979. With all the facilities that have been added year after year, we have much to be grateful for.

Sister Caitriona Mac Sweeney, Administrator of
St John's Rest and Care Centre, Knock Shrine

CHAPTER SIXTEEN

St John's Rest and Care Centre Knock Shrine

Sr Caitriona Mac Sweeney

Sr Caitriona Mac Sweeney is the Administrator of St John's Rest and Care Centre at Knock Shrine. She belongs to the Daughters of Charity and comes originally from West Cork. Before coming to Knock, St Caitriona worked in Nigeria, with GOAL in The Sudan and in Iran after an earthquake there.

The Rest and Care and Day Care Centre is a huge modern complex that caters for local and pilgrims' needs. Senior citizens from the area meet twice a week for morning tea and a snack, Mass, a four course meal (nearly five thousand hot meals are served annually), social activities and an evening meal. Alternative therapies, hairdressing and chiropody are also laid on. The centre is also the meeting place for well over twenty local organisations.

On average close to 200 large pilgrimage groups use the centre each year apart from the many smaller groups that make a visit to the centre part of their day. Many other groups are from nursing homes or pilgrims with special needs. Increasingly there are large groups from the Filipino, Polish, Indian and Brazilian communities.

You can contact St John's Rest and Care and Day Care Centre through the Knock Shrine Office at (094) 9388100.

Pat Lavelle, Manager of Knock Shrine

CHAPTER SEVENTEEN

Pat Lavelle, Manager of Knock Shrine

I was recruited as Assistant Manager by the late Msgr Dominick Grealy in June 1987. My duties are very varied and challenging – no two days are alike. My main responsibility is the day to day running of the 'business side' of Knock Shrine. This includes administration, upkeep of the shrine and grounds (100 acres), expansion and development of new projects, and promotion and PR for the shrine. Each year we welcome over a million and a half pilgrims to Knock, and it is important that our pilgrims find Knock a special place.

Promotional and PR work is about creating an awareness of Knock Shrine, as our national shrine and place of pilgrimage. It's about keeping Tour Operators and Travel Agents updated, who in turn will put Knock Shrine in their programmes and itineraries. I attend workshops and promotional events in Ireland, England, Europe and USA whilst working closely with Fáilte Ireland and Tourism Ireland.

We are always pleased to welcome journalists, radio and TV presenters and crews to Knock and let them see first hand what goes on in public and behind the scenes. Articles on Knock Shrine in newspapers and magazines are invaluable and an occasional feature on TV helps keep Knock in the news. Our website is also kept up to date with news and events. The story of Knock is ongoing and I'm always aware of the great faith evid - ent in the faces of the thousands who make the journey to Knock Shrine. I have fond memories of the late great Mother Teresa of Calcutta here in 1993.

Our shrine staff are a great team and it's the one to one contact that makes the difference, a friendly welcome and kind words are essential in a very busy world.

A great number of diverse projects have been undertaken and completed by the management and staff of Knock Shrine in my time here. Each has, I believe, added to the amenities and to the experience enjoyed by pilgrims and visitors alike. Regular visitors to Knock will recognise the developments that have taken place over the years but it is always interesting to list them out and to remember the great work that has been done. Projects completed include:

Presbytery Renovation and Extension
Shrine Information Offices (x 2)
Chapel of Reconciliation (including Architectural Competition)
Prayer Guidance Centre & Audio Visual (Refit of Old Confessional Chapel)
New Processional Route on Calvary
Apparition Chapel
Holy Water Fonts and Tree Planting
Churchfield Park Housing (30 houses and Community Centre)
Extension and Upgrade of Caravan Park
Knock House Hotel & Conference Centre
Knock Religious Bookshop
Refurbishment of Old Church
Relocation of new Office and Bookshop in Limerick
Refit of Knock Museum
New Archive Build and Set Up
Locating and opening New Office and Bookshop in Manchester.
Café le Chéile and new toilets at Knock Museum

KNOCK SHRINE OFFICES AND CONTACT DETAILS

Knock Shrine Office
Knock
Co Mayo
Tel: (094) 9388100
Fax: (094) 9388295
Email: info@knock-shrine.ie

Knock Shrine Dublin Office
Veritas House
7/8 Lower Abbey Street
Dublin 1
Tel: (01) 8733356
Fax: (01) 8733356
Email: dublinoffice@knock-shrine.ie

Knock Shrine Limerick Office & Bookshop
76/77 Little Catherine Street
Limerick
Tel: (061) 419158
Fax: (061) 405178
Email: limerickoffice@knock-shrine.ie

Knock Shrine UK Office
101, Deansgate
Manchester
M3 2BQ
England
Tel: (0161) 8192558
Fax: (0161) 8340744
Email: knockshrineoffice@btconnect.com

Knock Shrine Belfast Office
PO Box 210
Newtownabbey
Co Antrim
BT36 9DE
Tel: (028) 90774353
Fax: (028) 90774353
Email: knockshrinebelfast@gmail.com

Knock Shrine US & Canada Office
1275 Richmond Road #1409
Ottawa, Ontario
K2B 8ES
Canada
Tel: 613 829 5761
Email: knockshrineus@gmail.com

Father Frank Fahy CC, Ballintubber Abbey

CHAPTER EIGHTEEN

The Potential of Knock
Fr Frank Fahy

Maybe Knock, in our own hard times today, could hold the occasional forum or conference on our predicaments where the reality of people's lives can be discussed in the context of scripture and Christianity.

Fr Frank Fahey was a curate at Knock between 1975 and 1986. Msgr James Horan was parish priest at the time. Fr Frank is now the priest in charge of Ballintubber Abbey. It too is a place of pilgrimage.

I was based in Knock at a time of great change – the building of the Basilica in 1976, the apparition centenary and the visit of Pope John Paul II on 30 September 1979.

These were headline events but in a way they were a distraction from what was Knock at its truest. A place like the home at Nazareth, where, as the gospel tells us, Jesus grew and became strong. Knock ideally is a place where pilgrims quietly and without fuss grow and become strong in their own relationship with Jesus. They come broken, pray, bring what needs healing. Go away with hope.

The papal visit was both a success and a failure. It did get global publicity for Knock. But for the week before the visit there was no Mass in the shrine. Security. The whole place took a secular look.

We had dignitaries we never saw before or since. As against that we had people who walked from as far away as Mulranny (80 Kilometres) but never got within an ass's roar of seeing the pope. Parents and grandparents who loved Knock and all it stood for felt sidelined.

Knock and the big splash just don't match. It is at its best when we make contact in some way with the Lord, with the sacrament of Reconciliation, with Mass, with other pilgrims and with a shrine staff who are so important to the atmosphere and spiritual benefits of Knock.

The apparition was complicated. The figures of Our Lady

would have captured the attention first. Joseph's quietness would have been familiar. But they wouldn't have understood the significance of the Lamb on the altar. Or the importance of John holding the book of scriptures.

The pity is that the apparition at Knock came shortly after the first apparition at Lourdes in 1858. It was inevitable, but unfortunate, that at the start people tried to find the same meaning in Knock as in Lourdes. But Knock was very different .

For a start there was no spoken message at Knock. The figures in the apparition were the message. So those who looked to Lourdes to interpret Knock missed the point. Which meant they didn't pick up on the altar and the Lamb .

Knock was screaming the importance, the centrality of Mass. Christ as the Lamb of God who takes away the sins of the world. The call was to a faith with a strong central Eucharistic element.

They didn't pick up on the importance of book of scriptures John was holding. Scripture has been a huge part of Irish Christian art, eg *The Book of Kells* and of Irish prayer life. The Protestant Reformation and their emphasis on the importance of scripture over the rest of the Sunday service made Catholics go the other way. As the reformers made their ambos bigger, we made them smaller. As they made their altars smaller and plainer we made them bigger and more ornate.

A hundred years after the Knock apparition the Catholic Church did make a serious effort (in Vatican II 1962-1965) at restoring the place of scripture. A closer reading of the Knock apparition would have started the revival earlier here in Ireland.

They didn't pick up on Joseph. His stance of quiet prayer but also his vocation as carpenter pointing to the essential link between knowing the gospel and putting it into practice in the workplace, in sport , in the home and in the community. In other words, the social demand of gospel living.

Some might say emphasising Joseph as representing the social demands of the gospel would be politicising Knock. No, but it would be integrating and incarnating Christ into everyday concerns and their solution. Don't forget the apparition happened at a time of dire poverty here in the west. It was at a time when Michael Davitt was starting his Land League here in Mayo. The League was a strong reality among poor people.

At the same time many of those people also came to Knock and went away with the belief that God is with us but we have to do the rest ourselves. It was a time of hardship but fed with hope both from the Land League and Knock. Both the League and the shrine complemented each other and each played their role in inspiring people with a sense of their own worth as human beings and as Christians.

Maybe Knock, in our own hard times today, could hold the occasional forum or conference on our predicaments. Where the reality of people's lives can be discussed in the context of script - ure and Christianity. Themes like: Where does Christianity fit in the workplace?

During my years at Knock I was at peace. Every day brought its challenges. I suppose I learnt it is hard to move the church. We move slowly. We get bogged down in the ways we are doing things and find it hard to break out of our routine and be open to the possibility of new ideas, new needs.

Structures and buildings are fine and important but being able to respond as human needs change is more important. That takes respecting the gift of discernment. There have been developments at Knock that a little discernment would have advised not to get involved in. Having said that over the last 25 years good things have come in slowly. They should have been seen and acted on earlier.

Mother Teresa, RIP, with Monsignor Dominick Grealy, RIP,
June 1993 Knock Shrine

CHAPTER NINETEEN

The Day Mother Teresa came to Knock
Fr Colm Kilcoyne

The pain is part of the happiness, that's the deal.
T. S. Eliot

Mother Teresa came to Knock in June 1993. She was what today we'd call an icon. To be admired but almost too much beyond us to be imitated.

We knew some facts. She was from Macedonia, had done some of her training in Dublin, worked in the slums of Calcutta, set up a Children's Home and a mobile laboratory to treat lepers. One of a handful of living saints.

We knew some of her quotes.

To the eager young man who wanted to know how he could work for world peace: 'What can you do to promote world peace? Go home and love your family.'

'A life not lived for others is not a life.'

Her visit to Knock brought huge crowds. She spoke simply and powerfully about love of God and love of the poor and how they both were to a significant degree one and the same thing. And about her long hours before the Blessed Sacrament.

That was in June 1993. Fourteen years before that she had written the following to her spiritual adviser:

I work for Jesus, but he is absent to my heart. The silence and emptiness is so great. I look for him but see nothing. I hear nothing. My tongue moves in prayer but the words don't touch my heart. I receive the Eucharist with empty heart. I want you to pray for me.

She wrote again: 'I spoke as if my very heart was in love with God – tender, personal love. If you were (there), you would have said 'What hypocrisy'.

These quotes are from *Mother Teresa: Come Be My Light,* published by Doubleday in 1979. Mother Teresa had wanted all her letters destroyed, but the Vatican ordered they be preserved as potential relics of a saint, a spokeswoman for Doubleday said.

This spiritual darkness lasted for forty years. Which means that for forty years Mother Teresa went through a severe crisis of faith, what is called 'the dark night of the soul'. Not a loss of faith but a crisis of faith.

In 2008 a Fr Langford wrote about the darkness, the faith without feeling, that engulfed Mother Teresa for those forty years. (In the *Shadow of Our Lady* published by Our Sunday Visitor). He was co-founder with her of an order of priests.

As I understand it, this is what Mother Teresa did during those bleak years. She tried to experience – insofar as we can – the anguish of Christ in Gethsemane and on the cross (Father, let this chalice ... My God, my God, why have you forsaken me?). She tried to experience – again insofar as we can – the anguish of Mary his mother. She knew her own anguish over her 'faith without feeling'.

Each Holy Week was a special time for her in all these years of 'poverty of the spirit'. She prayed and tried to find some thread between Christ's passion, Mary's share in that passion and her own emptiness. One of the insights Mother Teresa got during those bleak years was that the passion is lived again in each generation. In her life for sure, but also in many other lives – if not all.

Her conclusion: The passion is now lived in people who are lonely or poor or unloved, or whose lives have no meaning. And like Mary, Mother Teresa concluded she too must be with Jesus where he suffers now.

That perhaps was the reason for doing the work she did and why she spoke so often about loneliness and alienation in lives today.

Just a few samples:

Being unwanted, unloved, uncared for, forgotten by everybody, I think that is a much greater hunger, a much greater poverty than the person who has nothing to eat.
Loneliness and the feeling of being unwanted is the most terrible poverty.
Let us touch the dying, the poor, the lonely and the unwanted

according to the graces we have received and let us not be ashamed or slow to do the humble work.

One of the greatest diseases is to be nobody to anybody.

This was the Mother Teresa who spoke in Knock June 1993. The woman who fourteen years before that had written to her spiritual adviser: 'I am in a spiritual darkness.'

All of which probably makes it ungracious to say this. That day in Knock could have been a most powerful witness for those who had journeyed to hear this special woman. To hear a woman of her fame affirm what those pilgrims were learning from their own lives, that often faith is bleak, that poverty of spirit is a terrifying reality.

Of course, it is tricky how much to say in public about what is going on in your own life. But that day of all days in Knock it would have been wonderful if Mother Teresa had looked out on tens of thousands of pilgrims, had seen the rows and rows of wheel chairs, had decided to step out of the icon role and tell us why, like the rest of us, she too knew what it was to be a struggling follower of Christ. Had led us through the journey she was making with Mary to some understanding of what the passion of Christ was. Why she believed the passion is ongoing.

The proof of that was right there in front of her that day in Knock.

Blessed Sacrament Procession at Knock Shrine

CHAPTER TWENTY

A Pilgrim People
Fr Colm Kilcoyne

How then are we going to reach God?
How, but in quietness and in confidence,
in the stillness and the silence?
How, but by learning to abide in a quietness within.
Joel S. Goldsmith

St Catherine of Siena says: Be the person God created you to be and you will set the world on fire. It is hard in the day to day world to find the time or the setting to look at what that quote might be saying to me and my life as a Christian.

But I need to try. Pilgrimage is an old tried and tested way of making the time and space. Curiously, pilgrimage is more popular now than ever. They reckon over 330 millions go on pilgrimage each year. From a few hundred at a local holy well here in Ireland to three million a day doing the Hajj at Mecca.

One and a half million go on pilgrimage to Knock each year. To varying levels of self awareness they all are trying to do what St Catherine says is the job of Christians: 'Be the person God created you to be.'

It is worth taking a look at how pilgrims go about that challenge and how well they succeed.

In the bible people who search for a deeper understanding of life are constantly being told the way to do it is to set out on a journey of faith. To get away from the familiar and be challenged by a new place, new experiences, new people. To listen to the quietness within.

Abraham is told to pack his things and set out for God knows where. He does. It changes his life to the point where today he is an honoured figure in Judaism, Christianity and Islam.

Moses goes up the mountain to get away from people. Instead he meets God and is sent down with the Ten Command-ments. Far from escaping people he gets a mission to tell them about the things that matter. Love of God, love of the neighbour.

Mary and Joseph have to leave home and journey to Bethlehem before Jesus can be born.

The shepherds hear an angel tell them that 'this very day, your Saviour Christ the Lord was born in David's town.' They make the journey; find the child and go home happy that 'It has been as the angel told us.'

The Wise Men get the call through their astronomy books. They journey furthest of all. They bring gifts fit for a king. They have a hard time of it but despite the harshness of their journey they persevere. They give their gifts, but do not return home empty handed.

These journeys and all true pilgrimages have a few things in common.

- They are a journey out from my usual life.
- I travel to somewhere made special because of a holy well or it is the burial place of a saint (Downpatrick), or it's a place of penance (Lough Derg or Croagh Patrick). Or because, like Knock, it is associated with an apparition.
- I also travel 'into myself'. This means that the strangeness of what I am doing makes me think more deeply about my life.
- I may or may not go on my own but when I get there I am part of a group of fellow pilgrims. I will need to make time for myself but I will also feel a freedom to talk to the other pilgrims. Share stories. Something about the place leads me to depths that would be out of range at home.
- I return home like the Wise Men 'by another road'. For a while at least different to the person who had travelled out on pilgrimage.

At Knock the first act of most pilgrims is to go to touch a stone at the apparition gable. Some say this is common to Irish pilgrimages. Now that you have reached your goal you touch some indefinite power that you cannot touch at home.

It is also a kind of clocking in. A way of saying 'I've taken a gamble coming to what is in many ways a parallel universe.' People walking around praying as if that was the most natural thing in the world. Grown men and women asking strangers where are the confessions. Seeing a sign for counselling or guided prayer, wondering will I give it a try and deciding 'why not?'

Sitting in chapel part thinking, part praying. Buying medals and relics for everyone at home. One for myself as well. A reminder I was here. A last touch of the stone on the apparition gable. Again, as some say, a wish, a promise I'll bring home something of the power of this place.

For others it is a kind of clocking out. Time to round up the gang and hit the road. To do that ritual all pilgrims seem to do – debate at length what car park is the car left in. Eventually we get sorted out and head home.

When we get there some of us may be a bit like the Magi and wonder what the whole journey adds up to. The things we saw, the thoughts we had. Like the Magi, some of us will have 'had the experience but missed the meaning'. Most, though, if we were half receptive at all, will have thoughts to chew over.

No one can say better what those thoughts are than pilgrims who have just finished their visit to Knock. Over the last few years the Knock Museum Curator Grace Mulqueen and the museum staff have invited pilgrims to write their thoughts before they leave Knock. Hundreds have. What follows in the next chapter is a tiny sample of these reflections.

Grace Mulqueen, Curator, Knock Shrine Museum

CHAPTER TWENTY ONE

Dear Diary

Grace Mulqueen

Grace Mulqueen is the Curator at Knock Shrine Museum. She and the staff of the museum have been asking pilgrims to record their memories of visits to Knock. This is a collection of some of the things that visitors have said.

Pilgrims write their memories just before they leave Knock

We are strangers here until we make the inner journey.

My name is E. I am here in Knock for the weekend. The weather is frosty but very bright as the sun seems to be lighting up the whole place.

The last time I was here the sun was the same, very strong and clear blue skies. That was 7 October, the feast of Our Lady of the Rosary. There was an all-night vigil and I just love being among other pilgrims in this holy place.

My first visit to Knock was around 1996. I was trying to give up alcohol and dope. They had ruined my life. I was 25 and found myself on a bus to Knock saying the rosary and singing hymns. I invited two other recovering alcoholics. We split from each other in Knock and when we met again in the bus they complained and gave out to me for asking them to come along! But I loved it.

Anyway I am 12 years sober today, thanks to Our Lady and my own efforts to pray. I have received many graces and blessings and learned to love and be loved. I am very happy.

God bless you all. There is hope. God will take you out of the darkness with his wonderful light.

From a young age I was brought to Knock once a year by my grandparents. There was great excitement as my brothers and I packed the car with tea and sandwiches and buns.

But the journey felt like forever, made even longer by constant stops due to my travel sickness. But that never stopped them bringing me.

When we arrived we were given money to go to buy medals and given a time to meet up again to have a picnic in the car park. My grandad used to have the keys of the car under the wheel for us in case we wanted anything from the car (you couldn't do that now – it would be stolen).

As a child you think everything is much bigger than it really is. The church was massive, the crowds were massive and my excitement was massive. The visit always came to an end with a lovely Mass with me sitting on my granny's knee. Then we filled ten litres of Holy Water in case we needed it during the year.

Back into the car and sick the whole way home again! Just to do it all again the following year. I'm nearly 25 years old now and still make the trip to Knock. Now without the travel sickness. *K.*

I am revisiting Knock with my daughter just like I always came with my mother who has sadly passed on. I'm praying for my daughter to conceive as she has lots of little problems. Our Lady of Knock has never failed my family over the years. We are forever grateful to her. *M.*

Today we have visited Knock and over the years I have always felt a lovely sense of peace and the joy of being able to make the journey. We love to come and feel we are stronger when we leave.

We have been to Mass and felt refreshed .We thank God that today we were able to be together as husband and wife – and happy and with love for our family, our son and daughter-in-law and grandchild.

We thank Our Lady of Knock for all our family and friends. This museum is worth while to visit. We have enjoyed it very much. *Husband and wife.*

I have found Knock to be a wonderful, peaceful and spiritual place. In these times of hustle and bustle it's nice to have somewhere like Knock to come to.

God bless all who work to keep the Knock shrine in immac-ulate condition. *Derry.*

I have come to Knock today to pray for peace of mind in myself and that of my family. It has been hard those years fighting with depression and the fight for the will to live. But being in Knock gives me the hope and inspiration that I need to carry on in life no matter how hard it is.

Don't stop believing! Our Lady of Knock, pray for me.

I have come to Knock shrine for many years. I have experienced a lot of cures but this one is very important to me. I was told I had a tumour in the mouth in Altnagelvin hospital in Derry. I came to Knock for one day before my scan. I put my face against the stone where our dear Mother appeared. Afterwards when I went back to the hospital the consultant was amazed. There was nothing there now.

I know I have been cured at Knock and I thank you dear Mother from the bottom of my heart. I could go on for ever with things I have witnessed but it would be never ending. *M.*

I have come to Knock this weekend to pray for direction in my life and to always know the truth. I have decisions to make that may change my whole life. I believe Our Lady of Knock will guide me in my decision making and that my children may benefit from my new decisions.

Pray that I will always take the right path through my life and that I will always do my best in every thing I do. Please God I will be back again next year. *A.*

This is one of my many visits to Knock. I really consider it to be a place of miracles. I can't help feeling an overwhelming connection with this place and believe whole heatedly in its power.

Journeys here have helped me build a much greater picture and understanding of what faith is. I also feel drawn to God, Mary, St Joseph and St John. Whenever I have prayed here my prayers have been answered. I was born on Thursday 21 August (the same date as the apparition) which makes me feel even closer to this place. It for me is so special and I feel completely safe here and at peace.

I feel honoured to be able to visit such a holy place and stand where the Blessed Virgin herself appeared. Even more so because of the tranquillity and love that surrounds all here.

I come here as often as I can with my requests and I fully believe in the power of healing and granting miracles. Yet I also know that even the smallest requests are heard and are never unheard or unanswered.

I believe this is the most hope-giving place in the world. Thank you Knock. *Xxx*

For me Knock is only down the road yet it is one place where I love to come time and time again. There is a feeling of peace and serenity here just simply walking the grounds.

I've just been at the Knock Youth Festival. It was spiritual and enlightening but was also a time of joy and celebration .

Knock will always have a special place I my heart. *D.*

Knock is a wonderful peaceful place to pray. No sound of bombs exploding; guns firing; crashes; murders etc. No television and negative news. Just sheer peace and quietness and a feeling of the presence of God and the blessed Virgin. *X*

Knock is a very peaceful place. I came here as a very small child when I was eight yeas old. I now have three children. Two leaving home for college . The third, the youngest, is nine year of age.

We just got up this morning and decided to go to Knock. It has been a very special day for us as a family. I am going home with a calm mind for the future. God bless. *S.*

Twenty-five years ago I first visited Knock with my late uncle D, RIP. He was a great uncle to me. Charming and kind with great faith. He also had a cantankerous element .

At this first visit to Knock uncle prayed on his knees for approximately 45 minutes. He told me afterwards he was praying to Our Lady to send the very best husband she had for me. I smiled and shrugged it off at the time.

On the eve of my birthday later that year I met R. Uncle, as soon as he met him, said we need to return to Knock to give thanks. R and I have been blessed with a good marriage for twenty-two years. As uncle was close to death he said we have unfinished business – to give thanks to Our Lady of Knock. Hence our visit today. Thanks uncle *D. K and R.*

My memory is of a most wonderful healing experience I had here in Knock. I am deeply grateful to God for helping me make a sincere confession for the first time in my life. When I came out from confession I wanted to punch the air. Tears of joy streamed down my face as I experienced God's forgiveness and love. Confession is a real gift from God to help us. Not something to keep check on us as to how bad we are.

Today is my brother's birthday. My family is visiting here today on his request. My first memory of Knock was coming here about ten years ago when my family was going through a difficult time.

Back then, to be honest, I didn't have much interest in my faith and I found the trip an ordeal because I really didn't appreciate it at the time. Now I see it was a major turning in the life of my family. I feel we have been blessed with graces from coming here. We now recite the rosary on a regular basis.

I would like to say the museum is quite fascinating. My faith has certainly developed a lot since my first visit but I still have a long way to go.

I would recommend anyone who comes here to spend an hour if possible in adoration in front of the Blessed Sacrament. Our Lady has promises attached when the rosary is recited daily. It is a great armour against the 'lad with the tail'.